Landscapes of
CORFU

a countryside guide
Seventh edition

Noel Rochford

SUNFLOWER BOOKS

Seventh edition © 2015
Sunflower Books™
PO Box 36160
London SW7 3WS, UK
www.sunflowerbooks.co.uk

ISBN 978-1-85691-458-1

Episkepsis (Walk 6)

Important note to the reader

We have tried to ensure that the descriptions and maps in this book are error-free at press date. It will be very helpful for us to receive your comments (sent in care of the publishers, please) for the updating of future printings.

We also rely on those who use this book — especially walkers — to take along a good supply of common sense when they explore. Conditions change fairly rapidly on Corfu, and *storm damage or bulldozing may make a route unsafe at any time*. If the route is not as we outline it here, and your way ahead is not secure, return to the point of departure. *Never attempt to complete a tour or walk under hazardous conditions!* Please read carefully the notes on pages 17 and 41 to 46, as well as the introductory comments at the beginning of each tour and walk (regarding road conditions, equipment, grade, distances and time, etc). Explore *safely*, while at the same time respecting the beauty of the countryside.

Cover photograph: Limni Beach below Liapades (Alternative walk 13-1)
Title page: Pondikonisi (Mouse Island)

Photographs by the author, with the exception of pages 52, 62-3, 64, 73, 78, 82, 87, 89, 93, 102, 103 and 115 (Mike Longridge) and the cover (shutterstock)
Maps by Sunflower Books
Drawings by Sharon Rochford
A CIP catalogue record for this book is available from the British Library.
Printed and bound in England: Short Run Press, Exeter

Contents

Preface   5
  Acknowledgements; Books and maps   6

Getting about   7
  Plan of Corfu Town   8
    with city exits and bus stations

Picnicking   10
  Picnic suggestions   12

A country code for walkers and motorists   17

Touring   18
  CORFU'S RIVIERA AND PANTOKRATOR (Tour 1)   20
  QUIET CORNERS OF THE NORTHWEST (Tour 2)   26
  CENTRAL CORFU'S VARIED LANDSCAPES (Tour 3)   30
  NOOKS AND CRANNIES IN THE SOUTH (Tour 4)   35

Walking (🚌 walking routes suitable for motorists; see page 7)   41
  Guides, waymarking, maps   41
  What to take   41
  Where to stay   42
  Weather   43
  Things that bite or sting   43
  Greek for walkers   44
  Organisation of the walks   46

  MT PANTOKRATOR AND THE NORTHEAST
🚌 1 Ag Spiridon • Cape Ekaterinis • Ag Spiridon   47
🚌 2 Imerolia • Bodholakos • Imerolia   50
🚌 3 Nissaki • Rou • Porta • Vigla • Kouloura   53
🚌 4 Nissaki • Kalami • Kouloura • Kerasia Beach •
   Ag Stefanos • Kendromadi   57
  5 Nissaki • Porta • Ano Perithia • Lafki   61
  6 Nissaki • Palies Sinies • (Mt Pantokrator) • Strinilas •
   Episkepsis • Sfakera • Roda   65
🚌 7 Spartilas • Mt Pantokrator • Ano Perithia • Loutses •
   Kalamaki Beach   71
🚌 8 Nimfes • Moni Ag Triada • Klimatia   76
🚌 9 Troumpeta • Sokraki • Spartilas • (Pyrgi)   79

  THE NORTHWEST
🚌 10 Peroulades • Cape Drastis • Peroulades • Avliotes •
   Magoulades   82
🚌 11 Paleokastritsa • Lakones • Makrades • Ag Georgios Bay
   Afionas • Port Timone • Afionas   86
🚌 12 Paleokastritsa • Lakones • Mt Arakli • Makrades •
   Krini • Angelokastro • Paleokastritsa   90

4   Landscapes of Corfu

THE CENTRE

13   Paleokastritsa • Liapades • Gianades • Ropa Plain •
     Sgombou   94

14   Sgombou • Doukades • Ag Simeon • Sgombou   98

15   Gouvia • Ropa Plain • Vatos • Mirtiotissa Beach •
     Glyfada   105

16   Ano Garouna • Moni Ag Deka • Waterworks Garden
     • Benitses   111

17   Benitses • Dafnata • Strongili   114

THE SOUTH

18   Messongi • Ag Dimitrios • Hlomos • Kouspades •
     Korakades • Petreti • Perivoli   117

19   Mt Ag Mattheos   121

20   Gardiki Castle • Korission Lagoon • Ag Georgios •
     Golden Beach • Perivoli   123

21   Kavos • Moni Panagia • Kanoula Beach •
     Ag Gordis Beach • Paleochori   125

Bus timetables   128

Index   135

Fold-out touring map   *inside back cover*

The Corfu Trail

Corfu's own long-distance footpath was opened in 2002, after several years of planning and hard work. It follows a meandering route of 200km from the island's southernmost tip at Cape Asprokavos (visited on Walk 21) to its northern termination at Ag Spiridon (Walk 1). The approximate route of the whole trail is shown on the touring map; the walking maps show where it coincides with routes in this book.

The Trail avoids heavily developed locations, and in passing through the island's rural regions, takes in as many of its finest locations as possible — some well known, some obscure. It links beauty spots, beaches, picturesque mountain villages, deserted hamlets, viewpoints, monuments, monasteries and museums. It follows quiet country roads, lanes and forest tracks, but also many centuries-old cobbled mule-paths — *the kalderimia,* once used by local people getting from village to village.

The route is waymarked with yellow aluminium signs attached to permanent features and augmented with yellow paint arrows, spots and blazes, these being the main markings in the mountainous areas.

Readers wishing to explore the Corfu Trail should obtain a copy of the excellent *Companion Guide to the Corfu Trail* by Hilary Whitton Papeiti (the route's creator), currently published only as a pdf download priced at 10 euros; see the author's website for details: www.corfutrailguide.com. She has also written other walking guides for the island which are available from the same website, but unfortunately no publication date is given for any of them, so we cannot say how up-to-date they are.

Over half the walks in this Sunflower guide share routes used by the Corfu Trail, so you will almost certainly come across Corfu Trail signing and waymarking from time to time. But *don't* always follow these waymarks blindly without reference to the text, or you may easily end up on the wrong path and walk further than you need.

☀ Preface

For centuries Corfu's magnetic beauty has attracted travellers, who have sung the praises of the peacock-hued bays, the hillsides drenched in silvery-green olive trees, and the emerald greenness of the countryside. And when you leave Corfu, these will be your impressions too. While time brings change, the pristine Corfu so beloved of Lear and the Durrell brothers can still be found, and this book tells you where. It turns the island inside-out and helps you find a Corfu unknown to most tourists.

The book focuses on walking, but it is not intended *only* for walkers. The car touring section will show you the best of the island, and the picnic suggestions make an excellent introduction to the countryside — many of them being at exhilarating viewpoints, reached after only a very short, leg-stretching walk from your touring route. You just might be tempted to return another day and explore a bit further.

Walking on Corfu is sheer bliss. You will be spoilt by a kaleidoscope of landscapes, and you needn't be an intrepid hiker to find these beauty spots. The walks lead to some of the most beautiful beaches you'll ever see, from the secluded pebbly coves of the northwest to the pellucid horseshoe bay of Ag Georgiou, the sand dunes of the Korission Lagoon and Durrell's favourite, Mirtiotissa. If you're adventurous, the rugged goat country of Mount Pantokrator will appeal to you. For strolls and short rambles, meander over the silvan hills or cross vast grassy plains flecked with flowers, surprise terrapin sunbasking in muddy ponds, plough through Corfu's few remaining holly oak woods, step across silently-flowing streams, and — in the bleaker corners of the island — listen to the echoes of abandoned villages.

In spring and autumn Corfu is at its best — alight with a spectacle of wild flowers that cover the colour spectrum. The fields and slopes are splashed with violet-blue Venus' looking-glass, flesh-pink geraniums, mauve anemones, vivid yellow marigolds, carmine cyclamen, creamy crocuses, sunflower-yellow *Sternbergia,* and elaborately-marked orchids. Even the thistles contribute to this floral splendour. And for fun, there's the squirting cucumber — touch it and see what happens!

Trees are another part of this finely-embroidered landscape. Perhaps the most eye-catching is the Judas tree in spring, with its dangling clusters of purple florets. In the country, massive oaks and twirling turpentine trees shade solitary dwellings and churches. Everywhere, the dark spires of the cypress pierce the island's cloak of olives.

Corfu has suffered a turbulent history of occupations and invasions — most recently the invasion of tourists. For four months of the year, the island is besieged by great hordes of them. This is the side of Corfu that you *don't* want to see. To know Corfu is to know the people. Out in the country is where you're more likely to experience the real friendliness — provided that *you* make the first move. So if you speak a smattering of Greek, don't hesitate to do so. The rewards will be immense. This is the Corfu of Lear and the Durrells. Taste the untainted rawness in the country, and not the synthetic spillage that follows tourism everywhere. There are today two Corfus and, with the help of *Landscapes of Corfu,* I hope you find the real island.

Acknowledgements
Heartfelt thanks to David Baker, long-term resident of Rou (see footnote on page 55) for his ongoing help in revising this guide.

Books and maps
Landscapes of Corfu is a *countryside guide* and should be used in tandem with a good standard guide, of which there are several available.

As a field guide to the island's flora I have used Huxley and Taylor, *Flowers of Greece and the Aegean* (Hogarth Press, 1989) and three books by George Sfikas (available on Corfu and possibly from amazon or your usual web supplier): *Wild Flowers of Greece, Trees and Shrubs of Greece,* and *Medicinal Plants of Greece.*

For information about the Corfu Trail and accompanying guide, see page 4.

Currently the best sheet map of Corfu, both for walkers and motorists, is the 1:50,000 map *Corfu* published by Freytag and Berndt; it is available in the UK from map suppliers and on the island itself.

If you've enjoyed Corfu, you may want to explore other Ionian islands using Sunflower guides:

Landscapes of Paxos by Noel Rochford features one car tour and many walks, all highlighted on a single sheet map (scale 1:28,000).

Walk & Eat Kefalonia by Brian and Eileen Anderson describes 10 walks and two excursions, all with restaurants en route — including their menus, local specialities and even recipes.

Zakynthos by Gail Schofield is a general guide covering everything from history to hotels but, in the Sunflower tradition, it emphasises the island's flora, wildlife and culture; the many walks and excursions are illustrated with both hand-drawn 3D and GPS-compatible maps.

Finally, for background reading, seek out the latest paperback editions of Lawrence Durrell's *Prospero's Cell* and Gerald Durrell's *My Family and Other Animals.*

Getting about

The two most popular and affordable ways of getting about on Corfu are by bus and rented transport. Even though the bus network is fairly extensive, it's not always convenient for walks and picnics. During peak season the buses are jam-packed and so sometimes do not call at intermediate bus stops, as they cannot take on any more passengers. And they often run late. For these reasons, *renting a vehicle is a good option*. Both circular walks and linear routes which can be done by using a car or bike in tandem with the buses are indicated in the Contents by the symbol ⛍. Often it is a short or alternative version of a walk which lends itself to this approach.

Car rental on the island is fairly expensive, and you will pay a lower price if you book and pay in advance, either with your tour operator or one of the lower-price international car hire firms with agents on the island. **Scooter** and **bike rental**, however, is very economical and two of the most popular ways of getting about.

Coach excursions allow you to see all the major sights in comfort, but they provide no opportunity for contact with countryside life. **Taxis** are another alternative, and sharing with others will help cut costs. Always agree on a price before setting out, and don't be afraid to do a little good-natured bargaining.

Those who prefer to use public transport should note that outside the main tourist resorts, the **local bus** network* (see timetables pages 128-134) serves the local populace, not the visitor. This means that buses leave Corfu Town for far-flung villages very early in the morning and return mid-afternoon. Some of the walks described end along these country bus routes. To catch the day's only return bus means galloping through some walks — not everyone's idea of a pleasant hike. The problem is exaggerated as the season tails off, when late afternoon buses from some resorts are discontinued. One way to overcome this problem is to stay overnight where your walk ends, which is not difficult outside July/August, since there are rooms for rent all over the island. Otherwise, you will have to arrange for friends or a taxi to collect you.

*See notes about buses and bus stations in the timetables on page 128; bus stations are shown on the town plan overleaf.

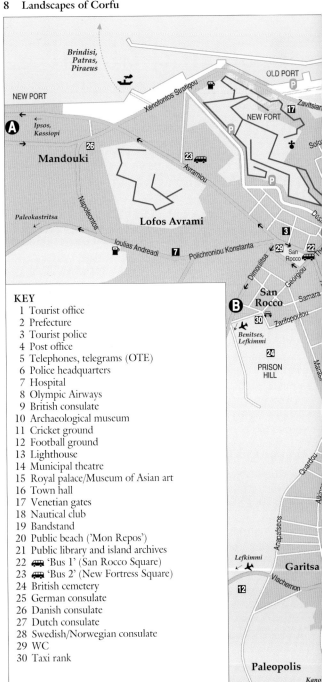

KEY

1 Tourist office
2 Prefecture
3 Tourist police
4 Post office
5 Telephones, telegrams (OTE)
6 Police headquarters
7 Hospital
8 Olympic Airways
9 British consulate
10 Archaeological museum
11 Cricket ground
12 Football ground
13 Lighthouse
14 Municipal theatre
15 Royal palace/Museum of Asian art
16 Town hall
17 Venetian gates
18 Nautical club
19 Bandstand
20 Public beach ('Mon Repos')
21 Public library and island archives
22 🚐 'Bus 1' (San Rocco Square)
23 🚐 'Bus 2' (New Fortress Square)
24 British cemetery
25 German consulate
26 Danish consulate
27 Dutch consulate
28 Swedish/Norwegian consulate
29 WC
30 Taxi rank

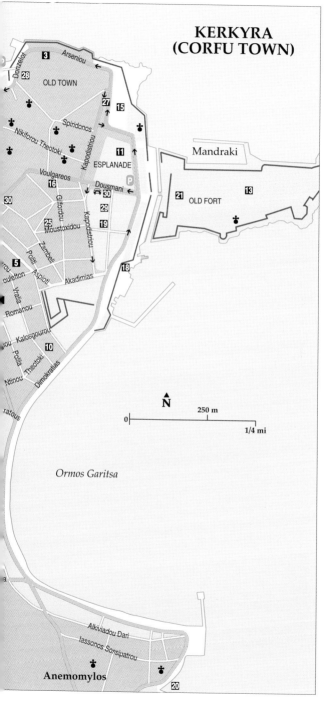

KERKYRA
(CORFU TOWN)

3 Arseniou

Donzelot

28 OLD TOWN

Nikiforou Theotoki

Spiridonos

27 **15**

Kapodistriou

11

ESPLANADE

Mandraki

Voulgareos

16

30

Gilfordou

Dousmani

30

21 OLD FORT

13

29

25
Moustoxidou

Kapodistriou

19

Zambeli

5

Politi Aspioti

rou
oulefton

Vralia

Akadimias

18

Romanou

Kalosgourou

iou

Politia

10

Ntinou Theotoki

Dimokratias

ratous

▲
N

250 m

0

1/4 mi

Ormos Garitsa

Alkiviadou Dari

Iassonos Sossipatrou

Anemomylos

20

✿ Picnicking

Corfu abounds in scenic little corners, many of which make ideal picnic spots. Ideal because they're far from the madding crowd, and unspoilt. They give you a feel for the countryside, yet you don't have to hike for miles. All my picnic suggestions are within easy reach, and most can be extended into short walks, should your curiosity get the better of you. There are no public picnic sites on the island, and none of my suggestions offers anything more than a lovely setting or a superb view. There are landscapes to suit all tastes — secluded coves, mountaintops, lagoons, olive groves, grassy fields, and abandoned monasteries.

All the information you need to get to these picnic spots is given on the following pages, where picnic numbers correspond to walk numbers, so that you can quickly find the general location on the island by looking at the large touring map (where the walks are shown in green). I include transport details (🚌: how to get there by bus; 🚗: where to leave your private transport), how

long a walk you'll have, and views or setting. Beside the picnic title, you'll find a map reference: the location of the picnic spot is shown on this walking map by the symbol *P* printed in green; 🚌 and 🚗 symbols indicate where to leave your transport. Some of the picnic settings are illustrated.

Please glance over the comments before you start off on your picnic: if more than a few minutes' walking is required, remember to wear sensible shoes and to **take a sunhat** (○ indicates a picnic **in full sun**). It's a good idea to take along a plastic groundsheet as well, in case the ground is damp (or prickly).

If you're travelling to your picnic by bus, be sure to update the timetables at the back of this book (pages 128-134), preferably by making enquiries at the bus stations. Remember that the timetables given in this book are for high season only and subject to change.

If you are travelling to your picnic by private transport, be extra vigilant off the main roads: children and animals are often on the village streets. Without damaging plants, park *well off* the roadside; never block a road or track!

All picnickers should read the country code on page 17 and go quietly in the countryside.

You have two choices for Picnic 11b on Cape Arilla. Either follow Short walk 11-2 (page 86) to this splendid view over the twin coves of Port Timone or, to enjoy a view north to Gravia Island and Cape Ag Stefanos, take the wide footpath opposite the front door of the church at Afionas. Up amidst the houses, take the second alley on the left, followed by a right and then another left. This path follows the spine of the ridge to the 'donkey parking lot'; there are sometimes a few donkeys here, munching straw — it makes a terrific photo. Continue on the path for another five minutes, ascending the rocky hillock over to the right.

You needn't be a picnicker to enjoy my suggestions; they make perfect 'leg stretchers', a good way to break up a tour and visit places the casual tourist never sees.

But if you *are* going to have a picnic, make it one to remember! Here's a short recipe for a healthy picnic: fresh fruit from the market, *angouria* (cucumbers), *domades* (tomatoes), a slab of *feta* (cheese), *mortadella* (a garlicky sausage), some *taramasalata* and *tzatziki* from the supermarket, some fleshy maroon olives (if you're into olives). Then pick up a loaf or two of fresh village bread en route. If you have a sweet tooth, add *baklava* (a pastry filled with nuts and oozing honey) or *rizogala* (cold rice pudding). Don't forget the wine!

1 AG SPIRIDON (map page 47, photograph page 48) ○

by car: up to 30min on foot	*by bus: up to 1h on foot*

🚗 Ag Spiridon Beach, northeast of Kassiopi. (Car tour 1)
🚌 Kassiopi/Roda bus to the Ag Ilias/Loutses turn-off.
Four good choices: picnic behind Ag Spiridon Beach (shade); follow Walk 1 (page 47) to the first cove and picnic beyond the bridge (no shade); take the track cutting across the headland to the old monastery (shade); or continue to the setting shown on page 48 (no shade).

2 IMEROLIA (map: reverse of touring map)

by car: 10-20min on foot	*by bus: 10-20min on foot.*

🚗 Imerolia, at the roadside (1km northwest of Kassiopi). (Car tour 1)
🚌 Kassiopi/Roda bus to Imerolia.

Either follow Walk 2 (page 50), to picnic on a shady flower-filled path or, for fine views across the bay (but no shade), start at the school at the northern end of the bay. Walk along the drive to the school for a few metres/ yards, then turn left on a gravel track. Just below the second house, turn right on a path and follow it up the ridge as far as you like.

Olive groves are pleasant picnic spots. This photograph was taken 20 minutes below Episkepsis, on Walk 6.

3 NISSAKI (map on reverse of touring map)

by car: 10-40min on foot   *by bus: 10-40min on foot*
🚗 Nissaki, off the main road, west of the Sunshine Vacation Clubs Corfu *(room for one or two cars only)*. (Car tour 1)
🚌 to Nissaki; get off at the Sunshine Vacation Clubs Corfu.
See notes on page 53 to start Walk 3. Picnic anywhere beyond the houses, under the shade of olive trees. Above the village of Katavolos there are stunning sea views over the Gulf of Kerkyra and Albania.

4a NEAR THE NISSAKI BEACH HOTEL (map on reverse of touring map, photograph pages 58-59)

by car: 10-15min on foot   *by bus: 10-15min on foot*
🚗 Nissaki Beach Hotel car park. (Car tour 1)
🚌 to Nissaki Beach Hotel turn-off (Kassiopi bus).
From the beach below the hotel, head either left or right along the coast, following footpaths along the stupendously-beautiful rocky shoreline. Shade of olive trees. Walk 4 follows this route.

4b KALAMI (map on reverse of touring map, photograph page 60)

by car: 15-20min on foot   *by bus: 25-30min on foot*
🚗 Kalami Beach; the turn-off is north of Nissaki. (Car tour 1)
🚌 to the Kalami/Kouloura junction (Kassiopi bus).
From the bus stop head down to Kalami Beach. Walk along the beach and take the path beside the restaurant at end of the beach, back up to the Kalami road. Lawrence Durrell lived in the restaurant building here when he wrote *Prospero's Cell.* Follow the road up the hill, then fork left on a track. When the track ends, continue on a path, to the exquisite cove below. Shade from a few olive trees.

4c KOULOURA (map on reverse of touring map)

by car: up to 5min on foot   *by bus: 10-15min on foot*
🚗 seafront at Kouloura. The turn-off is north of Nissaki; keep left and take the first gravel track down to the beach. (Car tour 1)
🚌 to the Kalami/Kouloura junction (Kassiopi bus). Follow the directions for motorists to reach the beach.
This is a pretty, unspoilt pebble beach, with shade from tall eucalyptus trees.

5 ANO PERITHIA (map on reverse of touring map, photographs pages 62-63, 64)

by car: 5-10min on foot   *by bus: not accessible*
🚗 near the church above Ano Perithia. (Car tour 1)
Head down into the village square, pass to the left of the two restaurants, and follow the footpath to explore the rest of the village and find a quiet corner. Shade of trees or abandoned buildings. You can also use the notes in Walk 5 (page 64), to follow the track some of the way to Lafki and back.

6 STRINILAS (map on reverse of touring map) ○

by car: 10-15min on foot   *by bus: scheduling unsuitable*
🚗 Strinilas, in the parking area on the north side of the village. (Car tour 1)
Descending from the village square towards Spartilas, turn right down a concrete lane just past the Strinilas sign. At the T-junction 30m/yds ahead, turn left down a track. Head over to the crest, where you have encompassing views over the northern hills and an enclosed valley below. Particularly pleasant in spring and autumn, but little shade.

7 SPARTILAS (map on reverse of touring map)

by car: up to 10min on foot   *by bus: scheduling unsuitable*

🚗 Spartilas village, on narrow streets. Don't block traffic! (Car tour 1)

🚌 to Spartilas.

Follow the start of Walk 7 (page 71). Picnic anywhere in the olive grove off the road, minutes above the village. For views over Ipsos Bay, you'll need to climb the overgrown hillside. Shade of olive trees

8 NIMFES (map on reverse of touring map; photograph page 77)

by car: 15-20min on foot   *by bus: scheduling unsuitable*

🚗 Nimfes. (Car tour 2)

Follow Walk 8 (page 76) to reach the abandoned monastery of Pantokrator, ensconced in a cypress wood. It's wonderfully quiet here.

9 TROUMPETA PASS (map on reverse of touring map) ○

by car: 15-25min on foot   *by bus: 15-25min on foot*

🚗 Troumpeta (limited parking). (Car tours 2 and 3)

🚌 Sidari/Roda bus; alight at Troumpeta, the pass you cross en route to Sidari and Roda.

As you approach Troumpeta from the south, the road to Sokraki branches off to the right at the beginning of the hamlet at the pass. Follow it uphill as far as you like; there are good views over the central hills early on. After a climb of 15 minutes, you can see the north of the island. No shade, so this is *not* a picnic spot recommended for high summer.

11a AG GEORGIOS BEACH (map pages 90-91) ○

by car: 15-20min on foot   *by bus: 15-20min on foot*

🚗 Ag Georgios Beach (via Pagi, off the Sidari road). (Car tour 2)

🚌 to Ag Georgios

Head left (south) along the track behind the beach, continuing as far as you like. Paths lead off from the track to beautiful, secluded sandy beaches. Shade of olive groves nearby.

11b CAPE ARILLA FROM AFIONAS (map pages 90-91; nearby photographs pages 10-11, 28)

by car: 10-15min on foot   *by bus: scheduling unsuitable*

🚗 Afionas. The bus turns round here, in the square, so park off the side of the road at least 100m below the square. (Car tour 2)

See notes beside the photograph on pages 10-11.

12a MT ARAKLI (map pages 90-91, photograph pages 18-19)

by car: 15-25min on foot   *by bus: scheduling unsuitable*

🚗 Lakones (the signposted turn-off is northeast of Paleokastritsa). The road is narrow; don't block through traffic. (Car tour 3)

For the best possible view over the famous Liapades Bay, follow Walk 12 from the 40min-point (page 92), climbing as far as you like. Shade of olive trees nearby.

12b KRINI (map pages 90-91, photograph page 93) ○

by car: 5min on foot   *by bus: 5-10min on foot*

🚌 or 🚗 to Krini (park on the left-hand side of the road before entering the village). (Car tour 3)

Head into the village centre and turn right at a street junction with a small tree in the middle. Follow the street, continuing straight ahead along an alley for two minutes, to reach the edge of the village and a

The sand dunes near Issos Beach, with Mt Ag Mattheos in the background (Picnic 20b, Walk 20, Car tour 4)

lovely stone-laid threshing floor with an outlook over the western coastline. No shade, so this is not suitable for picnics in high summer.

12c ANGELOKASTRO (map pages 90-91)

by car: 5-10min on foot   *by bus: scheduling unsuitable*
🚗 Angelokastro car park, below the castle. (Car tour 3)
The best place to picnic is in the olive groves on the hill opposite the castle. A path ascending from the car park towards Krini climbs up beside these groves. Shade

13 NEAR GAVROLIMNI POND (map pages 100-101)

by car: 15-20min on foot   *by bus: not easily accessible*
🚗 Ropa Plain, at the side of a track. Crossing the Ropa Plain from Liapades, heading south, turn left on a lane where there is a grass-hopper sign (see Car tour 3, page 32). Half a kilometre along, the lane reverts to gravel, and 100m further on there is a lay-by for cars alongside the track.
Use the map on pages 100-101 to explore the plain and visit the ponds. This is a beautiful, peaceful pastureland setting, as can be seen in the photograph on pages 32-33. Plenty of shade in this lush valley.

14 DOUKADES (map pages 100-101, photograph page 102)

by car: 15-40min on foot   *by bus: not easily accessible*
🚗 Doukades; park in the square. (Car tour 3)
Walk back along the road towards Paleokastritsa, then take the first alley on the right, to pass a church on your right. Now pick up the notes on page 102, to follow Walk 14 from the 3h-point, climbing the escarpment behind Doukades. There is a fine countryside panorama of the central hills after 10 minutes' climbing. Shade of olive trees. A 40-minute climb leads to the beautifully-sited chapel of Ag Simeon shown on page 102, but there is little shade up there.

15 MIRTIOTISSA BEACH (map pages 108-109; photograph pages 106-107) ○

by car: 15-20min on foot   *by bus: 25-35min on foot*
🚗 above Mirtiotissa Beach. The turn-off is signposted about 2.5km south of Vatos. Park at the car park where the road changes to track (in summer it will be manned, and you will have to pay). (Car tour 3)
🚌 to the Mirtiotissa Beach turn-off (Glyfada bus).
Follow the very steep track, down to the beach (very crowded in summer). The return is a real slog! Note: this is a naturist beach.

16 BENITSES (map page 113)

by car: 20-30min on foot   *by bus: 20-30min on foot*
🚗 Benitses (Car tour 4). After parking, walk on to the bus stop/shelter by the jetty.

🚌 to Benitses

Just opposite the bus stop/shelter — across the island square — an alley heads back into the houses. Follow it, using the map on page 113 to reach the waterworks. Choose your spot after passing through the archway (about 15min up the valley). This lush, overgrown garden is shaded by thick foliage. It's an intoxicating spot!

17 KOMIANATA (map page 113)

by car: 5-10min on foot	*by bus: 5-10min on foot*

🚗 Komianata. The turn off is between Strongili and Gastouri, on the alternative route for Car tour 4 (page 35).

🚌 to Komianata (Strongili bus).

There are two possibilities. For *views,* take the path that climbs above Komianata: follow Walk 17 from the 1h15min-point (page 115). For *bucolic charm,* take the path that descends from the village: follow Walk 17 from the 2h35min-point (page 116). Shade in both spots.

18a HLOMOS (map pages 118-119, photograph page 117)

by car: 5-10min on foot	*by bus: 5-10min on foot*

🚗 Hlomos, 5.5km south of the Messongi junction. (Car tour 4)

🚌 bus to Hlomos

Head into the village from the bus shelter/car parking area. Take the path ascending to the left, signposted for the church.

18b KORAKADES (map pages 118-119)

by car: 5-10min on foot	*by bus: scheduling unsuitable*

🚗 outside Korakades, at the end of the asphalt road, in a turning area. Leave the main south road in Argirades, following signs for Petreti and Kouspades. Keep left at the Petreti junction and right at the Kouspades junction. Continue until the road ends. (Car tour 4)

Head through Korakades and follow the lane leading out on the other side. Five minutes along you'll come to some abandoned houses. There's a tremendous outlook from here, over the rooftops onto the Lefkimmi flats and the hills of Epirus. You can sit on the wall on the side of the road, in the shade of olive trees.

18c PETRETI (map pages 118-119)

by car: 10-15min on foot	*by bus: scheduling unsuitable*

🚗 Petreti, either by the port or near the beach. (Car tour 4)

Walk south along the shore, cross two streams, then follow the path up and over the hill to the next cove, called Notos. A quiet, little-frequented spot. Shade of olive trees nearby.

20a HALIKOUNA BEACH (map page 122) ○

by car: up to 5min on foot	*by bus: not easily accessible*

🚗 Mesavrisi. Turn off for Gardiki Castle (south of Ag Mattheos). Go left at the first junction, then go left again, following the signs for Mesavrisi.

Picnic anywhere by the Korission Lagoon. No shade

20b ISSOS BEACH (map pages 118-119, photograph page 15) ○

by car: up to 15min on foot	*by bus: not easily accessible*

🚗 Issos Beach. The turn-off is in Linia, 5.5km south of the Ano Messongi junction on the main south road, just beyond a petrol station. (Car tour 4)

You can picnic in sand dunes, overlooking the lagoon and an un-touched stretch of coastline. No shade.

A country code for walkers and motorists

The experienced rambler is used to following a 'country code', but the tourist out for a lark may unwittingly cause damage, harm animals, and even endanger his own life. Do heed this advice:

- **Do not light fires.** Stub out all cigarettes.
- **Do not frighten animals.** The goats and sheep you may encounter on your walks are not tame. By making loud noises or trying to touch or photograph them, you may cause them to run in fear and be hurt.
- **Walk quietly** through all farms, hamlets and villages, leaving all gates just as you found them. Gates do have a purpose, usually to keep animals in — or out of — an area.
- **Protect all wild and cultivated plants.** Don't try to pick wild flowers or uproot saplings. Obviously fruit and crops are someone's private property and should not be touched.
- **Never** walk over cultivated land.
- **Take all your litter away with you.**
- **Do not take risks.** Do not attempt walks beyond your capacity and *never* walk alone. Always tell a responsible person exactly where you are going and what time you plan to return. Remember, if you become lost or injure yourself, it may be a long time before you are found. On any but a very short walk near villages, it's a good idea to take along a torch and a whistle, as well as extra food and clothing. ***Always take plenty of water!***

Other points to remember:
- at any time a walk may become unsafe due to storm damage or the work of bulldozers;
- strenuous walks are unsuitable in high summer, and mountain walks may be unsuitable in wet weather;
- do not overestimate your energy: your speed will be determined by the slowest walker in the group;
- transport at the end of the walk is important;
- proper shoes or boots are a necessity;
- warm clothing is needed in the mountains;
- always take a sunhat; cover arms and legs too!

Goats and shady olive groves — one of the most enduring images of walking on Corfu.

❋ Touring

Most tourists rent some form of transport for part, if not all, of their visit. Car rental is fairly expensive, but the rates become more attractive towards the end of the season (or you can pre-book a car; see page 7). Motorbikes are very good value. **But beware when renting**: many of the cars, to say nothing of the motorbikes, are not serviced regularly; breakdowns are frequent.

Before setting out, check the car (have you got a spare tyre, jack, enough petrol; do the lights work, etc?), and clarify the rental conditions/insurance coverage — in some cases you are not covered for travelling on unsurfaced roads. Don't take a car if you're not happy with it. Usually the internationally known companies are a safe bet, but more expensive. Always carry the agency's phone numbers (and after-hours numbers) with you.

During the high season, youngsters pour onto Corfu. All rent mopeds and motorbikes, many for the first time. The accident rate is appallingly high. Drive slowly and attentively. Also, in the countryside, beware of pedestrians and animals — roads are footpaths to them.

The touring notes are brief: they include little history

The beautiful setting of the Paleokastritsa Monastery, the jewel of Liapades Bay, is best seen from the viewpoint just beyond Lakones (Car tour 3). The same view is enjoyed on foot, from the slopes of Mt Arakli (Walk 12, Picnic 12a).

or information about the towns — all this will be in your standard guide book (or freely available from the tourist offices). Instead, I've concentrated on the 'logistics' of touring: times and distances, road conditions, and seeing parts of the island that most tourists miss. Most of all, I emphasise possibilities for **walking** (if you team up with walkers you may lower your car hire costs) and **picnicking** (the symbol *P* is used to alert you to a picnic spot; see pages 10-16). While some of the picnic suggestions may not be suitable during a long car tour, you may see a landscape that you would like to explore at leisure another day.

The large touring map is designed to be held out opposite the touring notes and contains all the information you will need outside Corfu Town. (Note, too, that much of the island has been mapped for the walks: you may wish to refer to some of these large-scale maps from time to time while touring.)

The tours have been written up with Corfu Town (plan pages 8-9) as departure/return point: most of the major resorts are within easy reach of the capital. **Tours 1 and 3 should be given preference if time is limited.** The touring notes *include* time for visits. **Symbols** in the text correspond to those on the touring map; see the key.

All motorists should read the Country code on page 17 and go quietly in the countryside. *Kalo taxidi!*

Corfu • Nissaki • Kassiopi • Ano Perithia • Acharavi • Episkepsis • Mt Pantokrator • Spartilas • Corfu

124km/77mi; about 5-6 hours; Exit A from Corfu Town (plan pages 8-9)

On route: Picnics (see pages 10-16): 1-7; Walks 1-7, 9

Road surfaces are variable, and most of the driving is on a narrow winding road. Heavy traffic on the coastal route in peak season. A motorway was under construction between Corfu Town and Kontokali at time of writing; this may be extended to Dasia.

Opening hours

Ag Merkourios Chapel (Ag Markos): make arrangements at the archaeological museum in Corfu Town.

Danilia Folklore Village (near Gouvia): 10.00-13.00, 18.00-22.00 daily except Sundays

---

This drive is the most rewarding on the island. Circling the sprawling rocky mass of Pantokrator, you pass Corfu's Riviera — an unrivalled stretch of coastline etched with idyllic coves. Olive groves, splashed with cypress trees, forest the cascading hills. Ascending to Pantokrator, the landscape becomes harsher. You climb into scrubby hills laced with rocky outcrops. A plateau, strewn with mounds of rock (see photograph page 70), leads you to the tiny mountain peak, from where you can see every corner of the island and over to the tantalising mountains of Albania. Heading home under a mellow sun, you coil your way down to Ipsos Bay and a picture-postcard seascape.

Setting out from Corfu Town (Exit A), stay on the seafront, passing the old and new ports. When you reach the main north road at a T-junction (🚏), keep right. The first 16km of this tour follows Corfu's tourist strip — a haphazardly-built-up stretch of unexciting coastline. But the bold presence of Pantokrator and the pretty offshore islands of Lazaretto and Vidos are some compensation.

Kontokali (6.5km 🏨🏠⛵️🚏⛺) is the first of the tourist villages; fortunately, the main road bypasses all of these resorts. The road to the Danilia folklore village★ forks left at the large Diella's Discount Centre (7km; starting point for Walk 15), just inside **Gouvia** (🏨🏠⛵️🚏⛺). Those interested in Corfu's history may like to see the remains of the Venetian naval arsenal near the marina. At the TSAVROS JUNCTION (9.5km 🏨🏠⛵️🚏) turn right; soon the floating chapel of Papandis★ is seen. Bypassing the resort of **Dasia** (12.5km 🏨🏠⛺⛵️🚏), you soon reach the largest of the holiday villages, **Pyrgi/Ipsos** (15km 🏨🏠⛺⛵️🚏); it stretches out for a kilo-

Moni Pantokrator, also visited on Walk 7

metre, beside a narrow pebble beach. Walk 9 can end at Pyrgi, the northern end of the resort.*

Continuing towards Nissaki, there are exceptionally good views back over Corfu Town. The road descends to **Barbati** (19.5km ⛰🏖✕), and you catch a quick glimpse of its pretty pebbly beach, set at the foot of olive groves. **Nissaki** (23km ⛰🏖✕🛏) is the starting point for Walks 3-6 and a good base for exploring the mountains and coast. Two superb picnic spots are in the neighbourhood (*P*3, *P*4a; photographs on pages 58-59 and 60).

Winding in and out of the folds in the mountainside, the obvious signs of tourism begin to dwindle, and small, handsome white villages speckle the ridgetops (🏖 at Kendroma). Pull over at the KOULOURA/KALAMI JUNCTION (30km 📷) and survey the scene. Below is Kalami (🏖✕*P*4b), still exuding some of the charm so clearly conveyed in Lawrence Durrell's book, *Prospero's Cell*. Kouloura (✕*P*4c), on the northern side of the point, also deserves its picture-postcard rating. A few palms are dotted amongst the cypresses, olives and eucalyptus trees around the shoreline. A small jetty with just a scattering of fishing boats enhances the setting, which is better appreciated from a viewpoint (📷) 500m further along the road. Across the channel lies Albania and its majestic peaks.

Climbing again, the countryside opens out. Another

*Just outside Pyrgi a road strikes left (off the first sharp bend) to Ag Markos (⛪✕), a detour of 4km return. Icon and fresco enthusiasts will find two churches of interest here: Pantokrator, which boasts the best-preserved frescoes on the island, and the nearby Byzantine chapel of Ag Merkourios★. Enquire at the local *cafeneion* to visit the former; to see to the latter you must make arrangements beforehand at the Archaeological Museum in Corfu Town.

enticing cove, splendidly naked of buildings, reveals itself far below the road. A collar of turquoise sea edges the shoreline. If you haven't been down to the sea yet, a detour (7km return) to Ag Stefanos (▲▲ ▲ ✕) may be just what you're waiting for. The signposted turn-off lies 3km beyond the Kouloura/Kalami junction at **Kendro-madi**, where Walk 4 ends. Keep left immediately after you turn off. Admittedly, tourism has already nibbled into this pretty sheltered cove, but it still retains a rustic charm.

The main tour continues towards Kassiopi. You begin to marvel at the wealth of trees in the landscape. In spring the floral splendour of the Judas tree, with its pink and purple clusters of flowers hanging from leafless branches, steals the show. **Kassiopi** (37km ✝▪▲▲ ▲ ✕🖵▵) is my favourite amongst the resorts. With its fishing-village flavour, it verges on recommendable. The remains of an Angevin fortress crown the scrub-covered headland behind the village. Many of the original walls and towers still stand impressively intact after some seven centuries. And it's worth stretching your legs by following a quiet road around the headland, visiting dazzling limestone ledges and tiny shingle coves. In autumn the ground is sprinkled with cyclamen, daisies and dandelions. Needless to say, there's excellent bathing here — head left on foot when you reach the port. In the Middle Ages, Kassiopi's church was the island's most venerated place of worship; it stands on the site of the Temple of Jupiter. Just around the corner from Kassiopi is the pretty seaside village of **Imerolia** (38km ▲✕*P2*). Walk 2 begins and ends here, climbing to the setting shown opposite.

Your next turn-off comes up some 6.5km beyond Kassiopi. Following signs for Loutses, turn left into **Ag Ilias** (▲✕🖵). In the village, keep left and uphill. Looping up through terraced hillsides, you briefly pass through olive groves. The islands of Othoni (the largest) and Erikoussa (the closest) come into sight, followed by the Antiniotissa Lagoon, nestled in a bed of reeds on a tongue of flat land below. The mountains of Albania, a long line of peaks, trail off into the horizon. On reaching **Loutses** (▲✕), the landscape becomes noticeably rockier. The village trickles down a ridge. Oaks and turpentine trees begin appearing.

Beyond Loutses, the untamed countryside shown on pages 62-63 envelops you: craggy, grassy slopes are littered with oaks, wild pears and holly oaks. **Ano Perithia** (51.5km ✕*P5*) hides deep in the folds of Mt Pantokrator. Nestling within the surrounding hills, this once-deserted village, shown on pages 62-64, is one of the prettiest spots on the island. According to the locals, it was abandoned some 50 years ago. But as recently as 70 years ago, it boasted a population of 3000, and *six* churches! Nowadays wealthy people are buying and restoring some of the old properties in traditional style,

Kassiopi, from the hillside below Bodholakos (Walk 2)

Attractive houses are a strong feature of Corfu's landscape; this photograph was taken on Walk 19, at Ag Mattheos.

and the village has been declared a Heritage Site by the Greek government. It's well worth exploring. Walks 5 and 7 pass through here; two tavernas currently operate in the summer, and no doubt there will soon be more.

Back on the main road, some 300m further on turn off right to the **Antiniotissa Lagoon** and **Ag Spiridon** (61km ⛺⛺▲🍴*P1*), an intimate cove with a shallow limpid sea, where I highly recommend you stretch your legs on Walk 1. Heading back to the main road, take the first road off to the right.

Continuing west, you head along a sea-flat, where almond groves compete with the olives. The short stretch of pastureland is quickly interrupted by signs of development (⛺⛺▲🍴🛒 at **Almiros**). In **Acharavi** (67km ⛺⛺▲🍴🛒) turn left at the sign for Ag Pandelimonas. Ignore the road off left 700m uphill. Cutting inland, you climb into the interior, hugging ridges and skirting valleys, always in the shadow of Pantokrator. Garden plots spill out across the floors of valleys. Dark blades of cypress trees cut through the olive-green countryside. The drawn-out village of **Ag Pandelimonas** (69.5km) passes almost unnoticed. At the junction just outside the village, continue straight ahead. Episkepsis appears, strung out on the ridge opposite. Entering **Episkepsis** (71.5km 🍴), keep to the middle (widest) of the three roads ahead. Walk 6 visits this charming village, full of colourful corners. A noticeable Venetian manor sits on the left in the village centre.

The route continues via **Sgourades** (76km), where comfortable old homes lean up against each other. Goats and sheep may cross the road. Some 1.5km past the village, fork left for Pantokrator (signposted for Petalia/ Lafki). The ascent proper begins, and there are fine views across the northwest of the island. Twisting deeper into the bulwark of rock, you come upon a basin of vineyards and garden plots. Rounding a corner, **Strinilas** (82km ✕P6) appears, set in hillside boulders and foliage. An enormous elm shades the square. The local wine here is medium-sweet and considered by many Corfiots to be the best on the island. Ask for a '*dopio*', if you want to try it.

Beyond Strinilas, you cross a ridge and lonely Petalia comes into view, set back in a bare stepped basin. Just over the ridge before Petalia, turn right uphill, following signposting for Pantokrator. Less than 1km uphill, pull over for a fine view over Petalia and the northern escarpment (📷). Mounting the plateau, you curl around rocky, scrub-covered hillocks. The landscape becomes more stark. In spring the stones and rocks are covered in flowers; just a short stroll away from the car you can find asphodels, saxifrage, marigolds, irises, fritillaries, veronicas, borage, and several varieties of wild orchids, tiny and ornate, often with the most amazing markings. Please don't pick the flowers! The panorama from the summit of **Mt Pantokrator** (88.5km ✝📷) is unsurpassed on the island. On really clear days, the toe of Italy in the north and the islands of Paxos and Antipaxos in the south can be seen — but during the hazy summer months only the whole of Corfu and the spellbinding sight of nearby Albania can be guaranteed. Ano Perithia stands out like a garden in this bleak landscape.

When you are saturated with views, return to the SGOURADES/SPARTILAS JUNCTION below Strinilas (100km), where you first turned off for Pantokrator, and turn left. Heading south, you're confronted with a splendid coastal view, taking in the bays of Ipsos, Dafnila, Gouvia, and finally Potamos Bay, stretching all the way to Corfu Town. In autumn the surrounding hillsides are soaked in pink heather. Walk 7 begins at **Spartilas** (101.5km ▲✕📷P7), magnificently sited on the upper inclines of Pantokrator. No other village on Corfu commands such a view. From here an almost endless series of S-bends drops you down to the Nissaki road (108.5km 🚌). Turn right, back to **Corfu Town** (124km).

Car tour 2: QUIET CORNERS OF THE NORTHWEST

Corfu • Troumpeta • Valanio • Nimfes • (Roda) •
Sidari • (Peroulades) • Ag Stefanos • Arilas • Afionas
• Arkadades • Ag Georgios • Troumpeta • Corfu

108km/67mi; about 6 hours; Exit A from Corfu Town (plan pages 8-9)

On route: Picnics (see pages 10-16) 8, 9, 11; Walks 8-11

Roads are generally good, but the country roads are narrow and sometimes bumpy. Watch out for livestock and pedestrians.

Once over the escarpment wall, you trail along ridges and dip in and out of lush valleys. An array of villages little changed over the centuries lies scattered across the countryside. The beautiful bays along the west coast provide good swimming spots — especially Ag Georgiou Bay, one of the most scenic on Corfu. If your return coincides with sunset and you can summon up enough energy for a 15-minute climb, use the notes for Picnic 9 to catch the island in one of its mellower moods: from the escarpment wall above Troumpeta, where no one colour dominates the landscape, the countryside takes on all the hues of the dying sun.

Follow Car tour 1 to the TSAVROS JUNCTION (9.5km ▲▲▲✕🖳), then head left towards Paleokastritsa, passing through **Sgombou** (▲✕; Walks 13 and 14). Leaving a pretty valley of cypress trees, turn right for Sidari and Roda (14km; signposted). Climbing through trees (17.5km 🖳), come into **Skripero** (18.5km). Notice the stately villas on the left, some with arcades. At **Troumpeta Pass** (23km ✕🖾P9), where Walk 9 begins, your views sweep out over the central lowlands of the north. And behind you, the Ropa Plain, the vast lake of pastureland shown on pages 32-33, comes out of hiding.

Descending into the north, the hills and valleys become more accentuated. Offshore lie the sharp-edged Theapondinisi Islands. Take the first turning right beyond the pass (making for Roda); then, just over 2km along (immediately before a Greek sign 'Roda 12', turn sharp right again, for Valanio. This narrow country road twists down into a luxuriant valley full of trees and gardens. Not far beyond an abandoned, enclosed hermitage, you enter **Valanio** (29km). Squeezing through this rustic village, keep right out of the square, towards Roda (indicated by a tiny sign). The road curls downhill into a wide, open valley, and crosses another stream. At the first junction you come to, bear right and head uphill through **Kiprianades** (31.5km ♱). An eye-catching church, with a verandah, sits on the left a minute past this hamlet. A

26

left turn at the next junction quickly brings you down to
the main road, where you keep right towards Roda. Half
a kilometre along, not far past a restaurant, fork right to
Nimfes (36km ✕*P8*; Walk 8), where a short stroll leads
to the delightful chapel shown on page 77.

Continuing to the main Roda road, head right. But
unless you want a closer look at this unimpressive resort
(▰▲△✕🍽⊕), turn left at the RODA JUNCTION (42km).
The road bypasses Karoussades (46km ▲✕🍽 ⊕), the
largest village in the north. At a junction some 5km
further on (🍽) turn right to **Sidari** (51km ▰▰▲✕🍽), a
sprawling resort on a long, but unremarkable sandy
beach. Caiques sail to the Theapondinisi Islands from the
jetty here (it's often a rough trip!). Half a kilometre
along the shoreline, take the first turning right (*not
signposted*) to the **Canal d'Amour★** (▰▲✕). At a

One of the coves at the Canal d'Amour

Coastline at Cape Arilla

T-junction just over the tidal stream, keep right, and park at the side of the road (in high season it will be very difficult to find a space). This beautifully-eroded clay and marl shoreline, etched with coves, is a superb swimming spot. The bare layered walls, fringed with heather and broom, stand out sharply against the turquoise sea. Local tradition has it that any girl who swims through the channel here — a short stretch of sea passage — while it's in shade, will win the man of her dreams. But tourism has long since taken its toll on this beauty spot.

Return to the main road and head west towards Avliotes.

Detour: From the PEROULADES JUNCTION (✕) you could make a 5km return detour (not in the main tour) to the impressive beach shown on the cover. To reach it, head through Peroulades (▲✕) and follow the signs for 'Sunset Cafe'. Sunset Beach (▲✕) is a narrow ribbon of sand at the foot of towering white bluffs. On your return through Peroulades, why not stretch your legs with a 15-20 minute walk to the viewpoint shown in the photograph on page 84? Park below the village square (leave plenty of room for the bus to turn round). Then use the notes on page 82 to start Walk 10 on Cape Drastis.

The main tour continues straight to **Avliotes** (58km ▲✕), an unremarkable farming settlement, approached via a low valley embroidered in green squares. Judas trees line the side of the road. At the end of Avliotes, fork left for Ag Stefanos. Haphazard development has scarred the countryside's beautiful rolling green hills around here. The pleasant sandy beach at **Ag Stefanos** (62.5km ▲▲▲✕), with its backdrop of cliffs, is best seen from the chapel. To reach the beach and its restaurants, turn right at the junction. For Arilas, the next stop, keep left. A gentle ascent takes you uphill to a T-junction; turn left. At the ARILAS JUNCTION (64.5km ▲✕▦) head right for the beach at **Arilas** (▲▲▲✕). Gravia Island, a sharp oblong rock, sits not far offshore. The Cape Arilla promontory rises boldly out of the sea to the left (photograph above).

Continuing on, briefly follow the seashore. A kilo-metre along, just over a bridge, fork right on a narrow road signposted for Afionas. The bumpy road winds its way up to T-junction, where you keep right for **Afionas** (69.5km ▲✕☞*P*11b). Keep in mind when parking that the bus turns round in the village square, so park *at least* 100m below the square, off the side of the road. Don't miss the unsurpassed views from the top of the ridge behind this village (*P*11b; photograph pages 10-11). Short Walk 11-1 (page 86) is an excellent introduction to Ag Georgiou Bay, a seascape of striking natural beauty.

Heading back out of Afionas, take the first right turn (a *sharp* right, signposted for Ag Georgios). The road is steep and winding. **Afionas Beach** (71.5km ▲✕) occu-pies the northern corner of the bay, which shows few signs of development. Continuing along the road, mid-way along the bay you climb above a cluster of beach-front houses. On reaching the crest of a hill, turn down to the right. The road briefly swings inland to skirt a swamp, before reaching the nucleus of **Ag Georgios** (73.5km ▲▲▲✕). Walk 11 visits the bay. About 1km along the beach-front, the way veers sharply back to the left and you head inland through a landscape of low-slung hills and valleys. Cypress trees make their mark on the countryside. Keep right at the junction, where a road goes left to Dafni.

Ascending into the pretty hillside village of **Pagi** (78km ☕), keep up to the right and, at the T-junction that immediately follows, turn left to pass through the village. Further on, another road joins from the right; continue along to the left, winding through olive-clad hills. The narrow country roads here are all being widened, so you may well encounter roadworks. At the junction midway through **Arkadades** (83km), turn sharp right. Some 1.5km further on, just past **Kastellani** (☕), you rejoin the SIDARI/CORFU ROAD, where you ascend to the right, to **Troumpeta Pass**. From here return along your outward route. Go left at the PALEOKASTRITSA JUNCTION, then keep straight ahead at the TSAVROS JUNCTION (98.5km), returning to **Corfu Town** in 108km.

Car tour 3: CENTRAL CORFU'S VARIED LANDSCAPES

Corfu • Paleokastritsa • Lakones • Angelokastro • Makrades • Troumpeta • Ropa Plain • Mirtiotissa Beach • (Glyfada Beach) • Pelekas • Sinarades • Ag Gordis Beach • Kato Garouna • (Ano Garouna) • Achilleion Palace • Corfu

114km/71mi; about 6 hours; Exit A from Corfu Town (plan pages 8-9)

On route: Picnics (see pages 10-16) 9, 12a-c, 13-15; Walks 9, 12-15

Roads are generally good, but narrow and winding. The road to Lakones is a series of hairpin bends and might prove unnerving for inexperienced drivers.

Opening hours

Paleokastritsa Monastery: 07.00-13.00, 15.00-20.00 (1.4-31.10); persons wearing bathing suits are not permitted entry.

Achilleion Palace: 09:00-16.00 daily

This is a tour that you can do at a leisurely pace, taking time out for some leg-stretching short walks, perhaps to some of the suggested picnic spots and then just a bit further... If you are more fond of walking than driving, break the tour into a two-day circuit and spice it up with the many possible short walks. You could climb the flanks of Mt Arakli, to one of the finest views in Europe, or check out the breathtaking perch of Angelokastro and the scant remains of its Byzantine fortress (Walk 12); stroll across the shepherds' pastures by Gavrolimni Pond (Walks 13 and 14); scale the scrubby peak of Ag Deka to the hidden monastery of the same name (Walk 16); wander down to the beach Lawrence Durrell thought the most beautiful in the world — Mirtiotissa (Walk 15). All these exhilarating and seldom-visited spots are accessible to everyone; for the most part, they are only a short distance on foot.

Follow Car tour 2 for 14km, where Car tour 2 turns right towards Sidari. Here continue straight ahead to **Paleokastritsa**★ (25km ⚓⛱🏠△✕⊕🅿), a top priority on every tourist's agenda. It's *the* resort on Corfu, and with this comes all the benefits and disadvantages of such a centre. At the foot of the Arakli Hills, on the edge of tumbling olive groves, rest six enticing turquoise coves, scooped out of the rocky shoreline. Tourism may have taken its toll, but no one can deny that the setting, shown on pages 18-19, is stupendous. Walks 11, 12 and 13 set out from here.

Following the road straight through the village, you come to the sheer-sided wooded promontory crowned by the monastery. (There are traffic lights at the foot of the monastery drive, which may involve a four-minute

The courtyard at Paleokastritsa Monastery

wait.) The blindingly-white building dates from the 18th and 19th centuries; however, the monastery was founded in 1228. The pleasant cloister garden shown above lies inside the gates. You may find the collection of 17th- and 18th-century icons in the one-room museum of interest. The monks here don't hide their weariness of tourists. Entrance is free, but one is expected to put something into the offerings box — they may even remind you to do so, should you forget.

Leaving the monastery, you have an excellent view of Lakones (your next stop), strung out along a shelf in the escarpment wall over to the left. Retracing the route for some 3.5km, take the first road off left, signposted to Lakones. The steep climb up a series of S-bends affords superb views all the way. Olive trees arch over the road like large umbrellas; dark pockets of cypresses lie amidst them. Neat rock walls terrace the inclines. Approaching **Lakones** (33km ▲✕*P*12a) — where a traffic light operates a one-way system, perhaps involving a five-minute wait — the coves below unravel, and soon the view encompasses Liapades and the coastal hills. One kilometre beyond the village, a balcony viewpoint (📷; with limited parking) provides the best spot to take in this magnificent panorama. From here the scars of tourism become minor flaws.

From the viewpoint take the first turn-off left, sign-posted to **Krini** (36km ▲✕*P*12b). Remain on this road until it ends at the foot of **Angelokastro★** (37km ■📷 *P*12c). Little remains of the castle, but the 325m/1000ft drops down to the sea from its perch are quite impressive! This Byzantine fortress is thought to have been built around the 12th century by Michael Angelos I. It was undergoing extensive restoration at press date, but should be open to the public in 2009. Corfu Town can be seen from the top; hence it was a good place from which to signal the approach of enemy vessels.

Return to the junction (lined with tourist stalls) just outside Krini. Turn immediately left (signposted to Makrades) and after 30m park outside an old school.

31

Walk straight ahead for one minute, then fork left on a concrete lane which soon becomes a stony track. Follow the track for about 15 minutes (or, if you're in a 4WD vehicle, just continue straight on to the end of the track; see the map on pages 90-91). I think this view (📷) — over Ag Georgiou Bay — is every bit as fine as the outlook from the viewpoint past Lakones.

Returning to the junction lined with tourist stalls, turn left. Continue uphill, past the edge of **Makrades** (🔺✕), to **Vistonas** (40.5km ✕). Then slowly mount the escarpment, snatching a view back down over Krini, Makrades and Angelokastro. Pink heather (in autumn) and yellow broom (in spring) bring life to these harsh hillsides in their respective seasons. From the crest a panorama unfolds overlooking both the north and the south of the island. Pull over anywhere along here and take it all in.

Remain along the crest of the escarpment all the way to **Troumpeta Pass** (48km ✕📷*P9*; Walk 9), then head right. Descending from the junction, you look out over central Corfu, rippled with wooded hills. Doukades, the next port of call, is the village snuggled up against the escarpment wall on the right. Some 3.5km down from Troumpeta, turn off right to **Doukades** (54.5km 🔺✕ *P14*; Walk 14). This closely-knit hillside village has some fine houses in its midst. Leaving the village, ignore a road to the right and another to the left; keep straight downhill. On reaching the Paleokastritsa road (🚰), fork left. Some 800m along, on a bend, turn off *sharp* right towards Liapades. At the junction just below Liapades (🔺✕🚰; Walk 13), turn left, coming onto the edge of the **Ropa Plain**. Heading along through farm plots and vineyards, you're soon passing un-fenced pastureland squared off by ditches. Some 5.5km along the Ropa Valley road, you pass the turn-off for Gavrolimni Pond (*P13*), signalled by a sign on the left with a grasshopper on it.

At the GIANADES/MARMARO JUNCTION, 2km further on, swing right and cut across the plain. Soon come to a three-way junction and head left. At the next junction, turn left and after 800m, turn right over a bridge next to the entrance to the Corfu Golf Club. This brings you to the outskirts of Vatos. Soon after passing a petrol

Ropa Plain (Walks 13 and 15)

station, turn right up the hill into **Vatos** (70km ▲△✕🚰⌕). Some 400m beyond Vatos, you round a bend and come to the GLYFADA/PELEKAS JUNCTION, where you continue to the right. The dark, wooded slopes of Ag Georgios loom above. This area is the setting for Walk 15, which crosses the island from west to east.

Although no longer as unspoilt as in the photograph on pages 106-107, **Mirtiotissa Beach** (🏊✕*P*15) is worth seeing. The turn-off is signposted about 2.5km beyond Vatos. Park where the tarmac turns to track (fairly large paid parking area, manned in season). The track ahead is far too steep and rutted for cars, so go down to the beach on foot (10min). In high season it will be very crowded. There are two tavernas not far above the beach, usually open from May to October. Five minutes past the beach the secluded Monastery of Mirtiotissa (Our Lady of the Myrtles) nestles amidst olive groves and pines. It is currently occupied by one monk who is deputed from Paleokastritsa; if he is in residence, then it should be possible to gain access to the fenced and gated monastery, to visit the church. *Please* observe the appropriate dress code!

From Mirtiotissa, the tour returns to the main road; turn right and then left at the next GLYFADA/PELEKAS JUNCTION. (You could turn *right* here to see Glyfada, another beach set at the foot of cliffs; you may find it less crowded than Mirtiotissa.) A steady climb through olive groves brings you into **Pelekas** (76.5km 🏊▲▲✕). Turn *sharp left* immediately beyond the first church reached on entering the village. This goes to a viewpoint called the

'Kaiser's Throne' (▲▲✕▣). In late autumn, the profusion of crocuses covering this peak may momentarily distract you from the wonderful panorama. You look across to Corfu Town and Pantokrator, down into the Ropa Valley and over towards the small mountains of Garouna and Ag Deka.

Returning to **Pelekas**, continue through the village, keeping left. Then turn right at the first junction. Travelling along a valley floor patched in vineyards, come to a second junction, where you bear right into colourful **Sinarades** (83.5km ▲▲▲✕). This charming village still retains its country character. At the T-junction (🚌) outside Sinarades, head right for **Ag Gordis** (87.5km ▲▲▲✕). Its scenic location has made this village a very popular spot, and parking is virtually impossible. To avoid the centre (near the beach), descend past the hillside apartments then, *just as the road flattens out,* turn left for Kato Garouna, winding high up the olive-clad inclines of Mt Garouna.

Everyone bypasses **Kato Garouna** (89.5km ✕), which looks unappealing on approach. But this cheerful little hamlet is bursting with colour and character. It's too small to drive into; park to the right of the junction and walk in. Turning left at the junction, swing back towards Corfu Town, circling the valley. Keep left all the way, ignoring turn-offs to Ano Pavliana and Ag Mattheos. The valley walls become steeper, with terracing chiselled out of the hillsides. At **Ag Theodori** (93.5km ✕), you come to the turn-off right for Ano Garouna (✕▣), where Walk 16 starts (a detour of 3.5km return). Ano Garouna also boasts a lovely view over the valley and a corner of Ag Gordis.

The main tour passes this turn-off and ends on a cultural note. Continue straight through Ag Theodori to the SINARADES/CORFU ROAD and keep right. At the GASTOURI JUNCTION, 3km along, turn right uphill and pass through **Gastouri** (▲▲▲✕). After 2km you reach **Achilleion Palace★** (🏛M), a whim of the Empress of Austria. This ostentatious palace (1892) was a retreat from the goings-on of the Hapsburg Court. After her assassination, it remained vacant until Kaiser Wilhelm II bought it, adding a few touches of his own. The expansive terraced garden, with its panoramic views (▣), makes for pleasant strolling.

Continue along this road to the coast, then head left on the main coast road, back to **Corfu Town** (114km).

Car tour 4: NOOKS AND CRANNIES IN THE SOUTH

Corfu • (Messongi) • Hlomos • Issos Beach • Argirades
• Kouspades • Perivoli • Lefkimmi • Kavos • Gardiki
Castle • Korission Lagoon • Ag Mattheos • Corfu

144km/90mi; about 7 hours; Exit B from Corfu Town (plan pages 8-9)

On route: Picnics (see pages 10-16) 16, 18a-c, 20a-b (Picnic 17 is on
the alternative inland route); Walks 16-21

*The main south road is well-surfaced but busy; the tour also follows some
narrow winding roads.*

The highlight of the tour is 'Lake' Korission — really a
lagoon. It's a unique, untouched spot, offering
something for everyone. Birds — of both varieties — for
the bird-watchers, flowers (orchids and catchfly) for the
botanists, a shallow beach for the sun-seekers ... and,
best of all, peace and quiet for everyone. Beyond
Argirades there is little of interest for the passing tourist
(unless you would like to see the salt pans on Cape
Lefkimmi). Kavos is included for the walkers among
you: it's a characterless resort, with absolutely nothing to
offer, but Short walk 21 is highly recommended.

The tour heads south via the coastal road. If you're
already familiar with this route, you may like to try the
alternative inland route described below. In either case,
leave the town from San Rocco Square/Platia Georgiou
Theotoki and Dimoulitsa Street, following signs for the
airport/Lefkimmi (Exit B). At the LEFKIMMI JUNCTION
(5km)*, turn left. Heading into Perama, you get a
glimpse (📷) of the Vlakerena Convent, joined to the
shore by a causeway, and Pondikonisi (Mouse Island).
This wonderful setting (see title page) represents Corfu
on every brochure. But from **Perama** (7km 🏨🏠✗⚑🏴)

---

*Alternative inland route: Keep straight on at the LEFKIMMI
JUNCTION. Five kilometres further on, turn left for Ag Deka
(signposted). Snake up the steep slopes of Mt Ag Deka, covered with
loose scatterings of cypress trees. The centre of the island quickly
unravels as you climb. Corfu Town and the Khalikiopoulos Lagoon lie
not far below. Three kilometres uphill, you pass **Ag Deka**, a cluster of
houses stepping the hillside, with a superb outlook over the gulf to
Pantokrator and Albania. Further around the now-sheer inclines,
Benitses comes into sight below, cushioned between hills, at the water's
edge. Epirus, over the channel, is a series of rounded ridges. A visit to
Halidata, Dafnata and **Komianata** (*P*17), charming pristine villages
with very old homes, is recommended. Walk 17 visits the latter two.
The turn-off is the first left beyond Ag Deka. Back on the main road,
turn left, to cross over the ridge and descend into the Messongi Valley,
woven in olive groves and garden plots. Down on the plain, you pass
through the small farming settlement of **Strongili**, then rejoin the main
touring route at **Ano Messongi**.

The monastery of Ag Deka (Walk 16) is near the alternative inland route.

to Benitses the coastline is built-up and unattractive. Colour in the gardens and the profusion of trees do, however, soften the blow.

Past Perama, you're just above the blue-green sea. Soon you pass the **Kaiser's Bridge★** (✘), a fancy marble jetty once joined to the **Achilleion Gardens★** (Car tour 3) by a bridge, of which a segment remains.

Benitses (12km ▲▲▲✘⊕), where Walk 16 ends and Walk 17 begins, rests at the foot of a thickly-wooded hillside. A new marina is under construction, and the village is trying hard to improve its image. A luxuriant wild garden lies deep in a valley, a mere 20 minutes' walk from here. If you're a walker, try Walk 16; if you're not a walker, take an evening stroll to the waterworks (**P**16; see notes on pages 15-16). Back on the main road, the remains of a 3rd-century Roman villa suggest that Benitses has been a seaside resort for many centuries (there is also a Roman bathhouse in the village). Beyond Benitses, development thins out to an odd hotel here and there. There is a lovely view of the coastline hills trailing off towards the tail of the island just before **Moraitika** (19.5km ▲▲▲✘➴⊕).

Approaching the MESSONGI JUNCTION (20.5km), you pass through another eyesore of touristic development. Keep right at the junction, heading inland. At the T-junction at **Ano Messongi** (▲✘➴) turn left, following the main road over a concrete bridge. *(This is where the alternative inland route joins from the right.)* Just over the Messongi Bridge, the road to Ag Mattheos turns off right. Keep straight on and leave the tourist belt behind. The road is wider and faster going, as you travel through olive groves, with the occasional vineyard and garden in their midst. From now on the tour turns off this main road at regular intervals.

The first two side-trips branch off opposite each other at **Linia** (27.5km ✘➴). First turn off left for Hlomos (signposted); on your return you will make for Issos

Beach from the turn-off just opposite. The ascent to Hlomos affords good views over the Korission Lagoon and, 1.5 kilometres uphill, a roadside viewpoint (📷) makes an ideal spot from which to enjoy the view. Entering **Hlomos** (31.5km ✕📷*P*18a), park in the small parking bay. For superb views walk a further 100m into the village and follow the signs up to the church, which sits on the hillside above the village. A fine panorama awaits you, encompassing the washed-out hills of Epirus, Lefkimmi Bay, and Cape Lefkimmi tapering off into a fine line. Even Paxos seems close by. Hlomos, visited in Walk 18, is not your typical whitewashed picture-postcard village. As you can see in the photograph on page 117, it has a touch of the farmyard about it; it overflows with character. Houses straddle a steep hillside crowded with a maze of alleys. Every house takes advantage of the panoramic views.

Back at the main road, cross over and wind along through olive trees, vineyards and fields to the dunes of **Issos Beach** (37km, *P*20b). Walk 20 visits this clean, wild stretch of seashore, which sweeps away to the right. The dark slopes of Ag Mattheos rise in the background (photograph page 15). You can climb the crusty sand formations rising from the dunes, five minutes' walk away, for uninterrupted views of the Korission Lagoon.

The next turning off the main road is at **Argirades** (41.5km ♠✕🛒). Halfway through the village, at a bright yellow kiosk, turn left (signposted 'Hotel Regina'). Dropping down through olive groves, you cross an intensively-cultivated basin. An abundance of trees — walnut, loquat, Judas, fig — grows amidst the olives. At the PETRETI JUNCTION, 2.5km downhill, head left to **Kouspades** (45km ♠✕). This *is* a whitewashed picture-postcard village. It's bright and spotless, with very old homes in its midst. You can park off the junction, where you enter the village, and wander up to the left.

Detours: From Kouspades there are three possible detours to visit pleasant villages or picnic spots (not included in the overall km readings). You could visit Korakades (*P*18b), some 1.5km along to the right — a sleepy little settlement facing abandon. The picnic setting here is a tranquil spot amongst the deserted houses, in the quiet of olive groves. Or there's Boukari (♠✕), a pretty seaside village on a quiet stretch of coastline 1km north of Kouspades. Petreti (♠✕*P*18c), a little further east, is a small and unspoiled fishing village with a narrow beach. The picnic spot just south of the village is in a pretty cove at the foot of an olive grove.

Getting acquainted with the southern tip of Corfu is best done on foot. The drive beyond Argirades is unexciting, and Kavos would be best avoided. But Short walk 21, which start out from Kavos, is highly recommended for everyone. It goes to an unfrequented corner of the south — see photograph on page 126. The touring route is straightforward: follow the main road through **Perivoli** (54.5km ▲✕🏕), where Walks 18 and 20 end. Then turn off (58.5km) to **Lefkimmi** (61km ▲✕🏕⊕), the largest village in the south. This neglected sprawl is really three adjacent villages (Ano Lefkimmi, Lefkimmi and Potami). Although this sprawling farming settlement can be bypassed, it makes an interesting detour (as long as you keep your eyes peeled in the confusing one-way system). Bird-watchers may like to visit the marshes and salt pans on Cape Lefkimmi, near Alikes. After crossing the picturesque Potamos Estuary, continue straight on. (But a left turn immediately over the river would take you alongside the river to a quiet beach less than 2km away.)

Continue through **Kavos** (66km ▲▲▲✕⊕), until you

The Potamos Estuary at Lefkimmi

reach a T-junction at the end of this resort. A sign for Corfu Town points to the left here. Keep right, immediately crossing a small bridge. About 200m further on, turn right again towards Spartera. (But if you want to try Short walk 21 to the ruins of Moni Panagia, keep *left* here. After 100m turn right on a gravel track and park. Then see notes on page 125.)

Beyond **Spartera** (70km ✕⌨) the tour meanders amongst the hills, passing through small rural settlements: **Dragotina, Neochori, Bastatika** (turn left in the village, signposted to Paleochori), **Paleochori** (✕; keep right at the junction), and **Kritika** (turn right in the village for Lefkimmi). You emerge on the CORFU ROAD at a junction (79km ⊞) south of Lefkimmi.

Turning left here, return to **Ano Messongi** and, just past the petrol station (96.5km), turn left towards Ag Mattheos. Some 2.5km along, turn left again to towards the 13th-century Byzantine fortress of Gardiki. At a junction barely 1km along, turn left. Soon an impressive wall and tower gate rise on a mound in front of you. All that remains of **Gardiki Castle** (◼) is the exterior octagonal wall with its eight towers. Walk 20 and Short walk 20-1 start here. Continue beyond the fortress, then take the first left turn (102km), to **Mesavrisi** (♠✕*P*20a) and the **Korission Lagoon** (700m further on a rough dirt road).

Circling the end of this shallow lagoon, you come to the beach. A causeway of grassy dunes separates the lagoon from the sea. The chaste beauty of the lagoon and the surrounding countryside with its reeds, fields and solitary dwellings, is a world apart from the usual olive-clad hills of Corfu. Grey mullet is farmed in the lagoon for its roe, which is made into *taramasalata*. A very rewarding and easy walk (Walk 20) goes along the dunes past the picturesquely-sited fish farm, over the canal linking the lagoon to the sea (photograph page 120), and on to Ag Georgios.

Botanists can while away the hours here, seeking out the loose-flowered orchid, *Silene colorata* (catchfly), sea stock, sea rocket, sea holly and various sea blites, as well *Medicago marina* (sea medick) and *Otanthus maritimas*. Bird life abounds here in winter and spring, but dwindles in summer. In winter you can see mallards and teal, and many waders — shovellers, pintails, wigeon, and dotterels. Even more birds visit in spring: avocets, on rare occasions glossy ibis, long-legged stilts, small waders

Walks 18 and 20: haystacks outside Perivoli

like the oyster-catcher, stone curlew, little egret, grey, purple and squacco herons ... as well as cormorants, gulls and terns — if you're lucky, a white-winged black tern.

From here return to Gardiki Castle and, just beyond it, bear left for Proussadi Beach, circling the foot of Mt Ag Mattheos. This part of the drive is my favourite: the gentle inclines harbour a vast museum of olive trees, with magnificent specimens arching out over the road. Narrow dirt lanes forking off left go to pretty coves, including **Skidi** and **Proussadi** (⬧✕). Keep right where a road heads left to Paramona (▲▲⬧✕).

Squeezing through a passageway in the hills, you reach the outskirts of **Ag Mattheos** (114.5km ⬧✕), a sprawling hillside village. A road joins from the right. At the junction that follows, turn left for Corfu Town. But if you've plenty of time left, I suggest the toughish ascent of Mt Ag Mattheos (Walk 19). The village centre, where you can park, is up to the right.

Descend through a landscape of mossy olive groves, spiced with thickets of cypress. A brief ascent follows, up a winding road to the hilltop village of **Vouniatades** (117km), overlooking the Messongi Valley. Dropping into this broad basin, you meander through groves patched with bright pink heather in autumn or sweet-scented myrtle in spring. Hills rise all around you, and villages peep out of the wooded ridges.

On reaching the KATO GAROUNA JUNCTION (120.5km), keep right and, at **Ag Theodori** (✕) pick up the notes for Car tour 3 from the 93.5km-point (page 34), to return to **Corfu Town** (144km).

❀ Walking

Few tourists realise the scope Corfu offers for walking, but this book has enough walks to keep insatiable ramblers occupied for a solid month. For beginners, Corfu is an ideal place to start: the scenic rewards and the countryside experiences soon become addictive. If you're not a walker, the friendly, quieter countryside will soon turn you into one. **All walks are graded and all walkers are catered for in this book.** The majority of the walks (at least in their short or alternative versions) are well suited for **beginners and/or motorists** (see page 7). If you want a *very* short walk, you need look no further than the picnic suggestions on pages 10-16. Hardy **hikers** should head for the Pantokrator Hills — they'll test your stamina. Although the majority of the walks are in the north, the book covers a good cross-section of the island.

Guides, waymarking, maps

Guided walks are only available on the island in the winter months, but you will not need a **guide** for any of the walks in this book. Most walks are easily followed, many being along country lanes and tracks.

Although some **waymarking** has been carried out, the walks in this book do not follow waymarked routes except where they coincide with the Corfu Trail (see page 4). While you may see waymarks (mainly paint dots) on some stretches of the walks, it is *important that you follow the notes in the book.*

Currently, the best sheet map of Corfu is published by Freytag and Berndt: *Corfu,* at a scale of 1:50,000. It shows distances on roads and tracks, contours, woodlands, and the Corfu Trail in its entirety. It's widely available on the island, but you can order it before you travel from your usual map supplier.

What to take

If you're already on Corfu when you find this book, and you haven't any special equipment such as a rucksack or walking shoes with ankle support, you can still do some of the walks — or you can buy some equipment at one of the sports shops in Corfu Town. For each walk in the book the *minimum* year-round equipment is listed. Where walking boots are required there is, unfortunately, no substitute: you will need to rely on the grip and ankle support they provide, as well as their waterproof qualities. You may find the following checklist useful:

walking boots (or stout shoes with thick non-slip soles)	up-to-date transport timetable
	spare bootlaces
waterproof rain gear (outside summer months	plastic bottle with plenty of drinking water
long-sleeved shirt (sun protection)	long trousers, tight at the ankles (sun and tick protection)
bandages and band-aids	insect repellent, antiseptic cream
extra pair of (long) socks	knives and openers
windproof (zip opening)	fleece
sunglasses, sunhat, suncream	plastic groundsheet
whistle, torch, mobile phone (the **emergency number is 112**)	small rucksack

Please bear in mind that I have not done *every* walk in this book under *all* weather conditions. For that reason, I have listed under 'Equipment' all the gear you might need, depending on the season. I rely on your good judgement to modify the list accordingly. Beware of the sun and the effects of dehydration. It's tempting to walk in shorts and to forget that, with the sun behind you, the backs of your legs (and the back of your neck) are getting badly burned. **Always** carry a long-sleeved shirt and long trousers to put on when you've had enough sun, and **always wear a sunhat**. Take your lunch in a shady spot and carry plenty of water and fruit.

Where to stay

If your holiday is going to be a walking one, the most convenient place to stay is Corfu Town. All the buses leave from there. Your next best choice, in terms of public transport *only,* is along the touristy east coast, anywhere between Benitses and Ipsos: Perama, Kanoni, Kontokali, Gouvia. Away from the tourists and the coast, Potamos is another good choice. Staying in Kassiopi, Nissaki, Paleokastritsa, Ag Gordis or Kavos will limit your walking to short walks, especially outside peak season when the bus services are limited.

Renting a car solves the problem of getting to and from areas poorly served by buses. But car hire has its disadvantages, since many of the walks are linear. (But remember that a car can be used in combination with the buses, or you can arrange to be collected by a taxi or friends who will take you back to your car.) You could also invest in a moped — they're cheap and will open up the whole island for you, inexpensively! Outside peak season finding a room is no problem (just ask at the local taverna or *cafeneion*), and making overnight stops between walks is great fun.

Weather

The kindest months for walking on Corfu are on either side of summer: April to June and September to October. July and August (with temperatures in the 30°s) are hot and sticky; the only walking you'll enjoy at this time is to and from the beach.

Spring is announced in April with warmth in the sun and an extravaganza of wild flowers, but the rain isn't over yet. By June a rainy day is considered unlucky, and in July and August, a phenomenon. Towards the end of September there's a freshness in the air again, with an occasional passing thunderstorm. In October it's time for a fleece and, as the month progresses, the cloudy days turn to rainy days. It's not the time for a beach holiday, but the haze-free cerulean sky and lush green fields, with their lavish pockets of autumn flowers, make this an exhilarating time to walk.

In summer the prevailing wind is the *maestros,* a strong nor'westerly which offers slight relief from the relentless hot days and gives cool, more comfortable nights. This gusty wind can last for several days. Another, but less common wind, is the *pounentes* — an ineffectual westerly breeze. A wind that will bother you on rare occasions is the *sirocco* — a hot, sticky, un-comfortable southeasterly that blows for short periods between July and August. It's recognised by its hazy skies. Fortunately this weather is not seen every year.

The prevailing winter wind is the *ostria,* a damp, mild wind from the south. January and February are the coldest months, with temperatures dropping (especially when the *sirocco levante* — SE by E — sweeps in off the snow-clad Epirus Mountains, bringing stormy weather). Ideal winter walking weather is brought by the crisply-cool *levante*, which guarantees clear sunny days.

Outside summer — mid June to mid September — be prepared for all kinds of unpredictable weather! Happy hiking.

Things that bite or sting

In general **dogs** are not a problem. On walks where one does encounter troublesome dogs, I warn you in advance. Pastoral dogs kick up a fuss if you venture too near their flocks/herds, but few are ever more than threatening. If dogs worry you, consider investing in a 'Dog Dazer' — an ultrasonic device which persuades aggressive dogs to back off, without harming them. You can order one online; various suppliers sell them.

Snakes are a more important problem. Fortunately only a couple are dangerous — the horn viper and the montpellier. The horn viper, easily recognised by its nose-horn and the zigzag or lozenge pattern down its back, is dangerous because it does not move out of your way! All other snakes are as frightened of you as you are of them. The montpellier, a dark grey to black fellow, is much less dangerous. Its fangs are at the rear of its upper jaw and unless it is able to get a good grip on its victim — unlikely when being trodden on — it cannot inject the venom. The biggest snake you'll see is the harmless, phlegmatic four-lined snake, which can reach 250cm/ 8ft. May and June is when the snakes come out to play … and September/October to a lesser extent. When walking in long grass, *always wear long trousers, socks, and shoes or boots — **never** sandals.* Take a long stick to beat the grass, and be vigilant around springs and water sources in high summer.

Scorpions are nocturnal creatures, and the only time you'll encounter them is when you move logs or rocks. Do so carefully. Their sting is not dangerous, just painful.

Bees and **wasps** abound in summer, particularly around water. Approach all water sources and ponds, etc with care. If you're allergic to stings, make sure you have the necessary pills with you.

Perhaps the biggest nuisance (but only in summer) is the **horse-fly**. Keeping them off you is more exhausting than the walk itself. Long trousers and long-sleeved shirts lessen the problem. Avoid **ticks** by wearing long socks.

You'll also encounter, or hear, lots of **hunters**. They blast away at anything that moves or flies. Don't be afraid to shout and let them know you're around!

The **drinking water** in village fountains is safe but, in outlying areas, **wells have been polluted** by fertilisers.

Greek for walkers

In the major tourist areas you hardly need to know any Greek at all, but once you are out in the countryside a few words of the language will be helpful. Here's one way to ask directions in Greek *and understand the answers you get!* First memorise the few 'key' and 'secondary' questions given below. Then, always follow your key question with a **second question demanding a yes *(ne)* or no *(ochi)* answer**. Greeks invariably raise their heads to say 'no', which looks to us like the beginning of a 'yes'! By the way, 'ochi' (no) might be pronounced as **o**-hee, o-shee or even **oi**-ee.

Following are the two most likely situations in which you may have to use some Greek. The dots (…) show where you will fill in the name of your destination. Ask locally for help with pronunciation; accented syllables are shown in the Index beginning on page 135.

■ Asking the way
The key questions

English	*Approximate Greek pronunciation*
Hello, good day, greetings	**Hair**-i-tay
Please —	**Sas** pa-ra-ka-**loh** —
where is	**pou-ee**-nay
the road that goes to …?	o **thro**-mo stoh …?
the footpath that goes to …?	ee mono-**pati** stoh …?
the bus stop?	ee **stass**is?
Many thanks.	Eff-hah-ree-**stoh** po-li.

Secondary question leading to a yes/no answer

English	*Approximate Greek pronunciation*
Is it here?	**Ee**-nay cth-**o**?
Is it there?	**Ee**-nay eh-**kee**?
Is it straight ahead?	**Ee**-nay kat-eff-**thia**?
Is it behind?	**Ee**-nay **pee**-so?
Is it to the right?	**Ee**-nay thex-**ya**?
Is it to the left?	**Ee**-nay aris-teh-**rah**?
Is it above?	**Ee**-nay eh-**pa**-no?
Is it below?	**Ee**-nay **kah**-to?

■ Asking a taxi driver to take you somewhere and return for you, or asking a taxi driver to collect you somewhere

English	*Approximate Greek pronunciation*
Please —	**Sas** pa-ra-ka-**loh** —
would you take us to … ?	tha **pah**-reh mas stoh … ?
Come and pick us up	**El**-la na mas **pah**-reh-teh
at … (place) at … (time)	apo … stees …

(Instead of memorising the hours of the day, simply point out on your watch the time you wish to be collected.)

Since you may have to rely on taxis for some walks, you might ask your hotel to find a driver who speaks good English. (In the resorts, all taxi drivers speak at least some English.) I'd also recommend you take an inexpensive phrase book. An especially useful book is Tom Stone's *Essential Greek Handbook,* which you should be able to find on the web. It has many key phrases and pronunciation hints, plus a wealth of practical information.

Organisation of the walks

The 21 main walks in this book are grouped in four general areas: around Mt Pantokrator and the northeast, the northwest, the centre of the island, and the south. You might begin by considering the large fold-out touring map inside the back cover. Here you can see at a glance the overall terrain, the road network, and the orientation of the walking maps in the text. Quickly flipping through the book, you'll find that there's at least one photograph for each walk.

Having selected one or two potential excursions from the map and the photographs, look over the planning information at the beginning of each walk. Here you'll find walking times, grade, equipment, and how to get there/return. If the grade and equipment specifications are beyond your scope, don't despair! *There's almost always a short or alternative version of a walk* and, in most cases, these are less demanding of agility and equipment. If it still looks too strenuous for you, turn to pages 10-16, where the picnic suggestions allow you to savour a walk's special landscape with minimum effort.

The text of each walk begins with an introduction to the overall landscape and then describes the route in detail. The **large-scale maps** (all 1:50,000 and all with north at the top) have been drawn to show current routes and key landmarks. **Times** are given for reaching certain landmarks. To work out how your walking pace compares with mine, start out with a couple of the easier walks. This is particularly important if you are relying on public transport at the end of a hike. You'll soon see how your pace compares with mine. Since I always do my research out of season when it's cooler (and cheaper!), it would be a good idea when planning to ***add up to 50% to my walking times***, to allow for dawdling … *and the heat!*

Many of the **symbols** used on the walking maps are self-explanatory, but below is a key.

▬▬▬ major road	⛪ church, monastery	⊣ cemetery
▭▭▭ other wide road	🖻 best views	⚡ danger; vertigo
▭▭▭ minor road	🚌 bus stop	✿ garden
─── track	🚗 car parking	⚑ military area
- - - - path or steps	*P* picnic (see page 10)	❏† signpost.shrine
2→ main walk	⚲ spring, tank, etc	■□ building.shed/corral
2→ alternative route	⚒ quarry	■ castle
-(CT)-- Corfu Trail	⚽ football ground	📖 page reference

Walk 1: AG SPIRIDON • CAPE EKATERINIS • AG SPIRIDON

Distance/time: 4.5km/2.8mi; 1h30min

Grade: easy, but the coastal path is very rocky, and there is little shade

Equipment: boots or stout shoes with good ankle support, sunhat, suncream, sunglasses, swimwear, picnic, water

How to get there and return: 🚌 to/from the beach or the church at Ag Spiridon

Alternative walk: Ag Ilias junction — Ag Spiridon — Cape Ekaterinis — Portes junction: 7km/4.3mi; 2h. Grade and equipment as above; easy descent to begin. 🚌 to the Ag Ilias/Loutses junction (Corfu to Loutses bus; journey time 1h15min, or Kassiopi to Sidari bus; journey time 10min). From the bus stop, walk northeast downhill and take the first turn-off to the right; keep straight downhill to the beach, then pick up the main walk below. Follow it to the 45min-point, then use the map below to follow the Corfu Trail to the bus stop at the Portes junction, 35 minutes along, for a Kassiopi to Roda 🚌.

This short walk is suitable for everyone, from kids to grannies. If you find the rocky coastal path hard going, you can switch to the track a short way inland. Cape Ekaterinis, with its lagoon, tidal streams, and small coves, is very picturesque — and tranquil outside high season. Pines and cypress trees also make a pleasant change from the ubiquitous olive.

The walk starts from the CHURCH at **Ag Spiridon** (which is the northern termination of the 200km Corfu Trail): continue west behind the main beach. This headland is refreshingly unspoilt, and the shallow sandy beach is ideal for children. The **Antiniotissa Lagoon** lies behind the beach, and you soon cross a small bridge over a tidal stream. This very pretty spot, overlooking the lagoon to the inland hills, is quite untypical of Corfu.

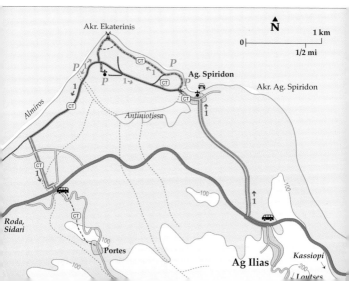

Immediately over the bridge, by the rail, descend to the right, to head along the edge of the water, which is the lagoon's first outlet to the sea. (But if it's high tide, you will have to continue along the gravel road for a few metres, then follow the slightly-overgrown path that strikes off into the scrub, curving slowly to the right to return to the shoreline.)

View inland from the lagoon's second outlet to the sea (Picnic 1)

Once at the water's edge, pick up a path heading round the promontory. A ribbon of pale green water borders the limestone shoreline. Within the first **20min** you're crossing the first cove (Picnic 1). But don't plan to swim here: a bar of rocks cuts across this cove near the shore.

Rejoin the coastal path at the far end of the beach. Quite different from the area not far to the south, this coastline is flat and bare of trees. Inland, the massive mound of Pantokrator bulges out of the landscape. Across the straights, in Albania, the coastal hills climb into mountains. The path continues around the coast, passing a BEACON at the tip of **Cape Ekaterinis** (**35min**), the northernmost point on Corfu.

Terebinth trees encroach on the shoreline as you round the headland, and a second cove comes into sight. From here one can see straight along the coast as it curves towards Cape Astrakeri, and Roda doesn't seem very far away. The ruins of an old monastery are visible, in a clump of trees up ahead. A few minutes later you cross the SECOND COVE. Here you pick up a track which takes you to a JUNCTION: turn right. Crossing a small rise, you look down on some sea walls built of rock (probably to protect the outlet channel ahead); to the right is **Almiros Beach** — an endless stretch of sand. Minutes later come to the lagoon's second outlet to the sea (**45min**), with a footbridge across to Almiros — another setting for Picnic 1 (see opposite). This is where the main walk turns back. *(For the Alternative walk, refer to the map to walk on from here to the bus stop at the Portes turn-off, 35 minutes away; the turn-off is slightly to the right of where you meet the main road. At time of writing this was the route of the Corfu Trail.)*

The main walk returns from the outlet to the junction, where you keep straight ahead. Barely 100m/yds beyond the junction, you come to a grove of eucalyptus on the right. Take the path (which may be somewhat over-grown) through the grove, to explore the ABANDONED MONASTERY. But take care around the old walls and the steps: both have crumbled away in places.

Then return to the main track and follow it back to Ag Spiridon, ignoring all side-tracks. Beyond the monas-tery the way is briefly flanked by tall cypress trees, and avenues of pine lie behind them. It's a cool few minutes. Finally you cross an open, treeless flat area covered in ferns, before reaching **Ag Spiridon** (**1h30min**).

Walk 2: IMEROLIA • BODHOLAKOS • IMEROLIA

See map on reverse of touring map; see also photograph page 23

Distance/time: 4.25km/2.6mi; 1h40min

Grade: moderate, but with a steep climb at the start (ascent/descent of 350m/1150ft). *Beware:* at the isolated farm of Kato Bodholakos there *may be* very vicious dogs, although when the walk was last checked in summer 2014, there were no dogs around.

Equipment: walking boots, long socks, sunhat, suncream, long-sleeved shirt, fleece, raingear, picnic, water, Dog Dazer (see page 44)

How to get there and return: ⛟ to/from Imerolia (park off the seaward side of the main road just east of the village) or Ag Ilias/Loutses 🚌 to/from Imerolia. Alight on the east side of the village, where a stony track forks off left between a bus shelter and the first house on the left as you approach from Kassiopi.

This walk is Kassiopi's best kept secret. Not only does it have one of the prettiest footpaths on the island, but in spring it's a garden full of colour. The whole route is drenched with flowers. And not only are there fine views on offer, but a deserted hamlet is an added bonus. This short hike is best saved for the evening, when it's cooler and the light is at its best. Don't miss it.

The walk starts on the east side of the village of **Imerolia**. Head up a stony track leading into the valley behind the village: the route begins next to the BUS SHELTER. A minute along, after a chicken coop, turn left off the track (which continues over a stream bed), and ascend a path. The path is lined with a profusion of colourful flowers (Picnic 2). The valley floor, crammed with trees, is fresh and verdant; the valley walls lean back steeply on either side. The path crosses the stream bed (**5min**) and runs alongside the track, before climbing more steeply up the left side of the valley. It then descends gently, passes through a shady tunnel of trees, and crosses the stream bed again. A minute later (**15min**), take the well-used stony path climbing steeply on the right. A strenuous climb lies ahead. Within minutes you pass through a little wood of kermes oaks, the path ascending in zigzags.

A couple of minutes further along, the path flattens out, and you pass alongside the remains of a STONE PEN on the left. The path forks from time to time, but soon joins up again. Now in the higher reaches of the valley, five minutes from the pen, leave the valley floor and ascend the low crest on the left, ignoring a path to the

Bodholakos

50

right (which leads to a well below an walled-in olive grove). Animal paths around here will confuse you but, if you walk in a curving arc to the left, within just one minute you should find yourselves to the right of an OLIVE GROVE set behind stone walls. Remaining alongside the wall, continue up to the right, ignoring all paths forking off right.

Reaching the end of the wall, clamber over some large stones, to join a farm track. Turn left to reach the large farmhouse. This is part of the tiny outpost of **Bodholakos** (**45min**). This hamlet is no longer inhabited, but there are well-tended vegetable plots, and chicken coops adorn the buildings. The old buildings themselves serve as pens for livestock now. Continue up the path, passing to the left of the house. Another homestead, equally large, appears behind it. And between the two, you'll find a lovely big oak tree to sit under and contemplate your peaceful surroundings and the stupendous view. (But the best viewpoint is five minutes further uphill.)

To continue the walk, stand facing this SECOND HOUSE. There's a chicken pen and a small shed a few metres to the right of it. Between the pen and the shed is a large clump of rock on the hillside ahead. That's your target. Follow the path that ascends to the right of the little shed, keeping straight up and aiming for the right-hand side of the clump of rock. The path then swings left to ascend up over the CLUMP OF ROCK (**50min**). Here's where you can pause for a while and soak up the magnificent panorama that lies before you, with the bare mountains of Albania filling in the backdrop. Just below

you can see a corner of Kassiopi; to the right is Avlaki's bay, and behind that the almost-hidden Lake Butrinto in Albania. Sitting here until late evening, under a softening sun, is therapeutic beyond words.

When you want to continue, head back down to the lower farmhouse. You can now enjoy a lovely stroll along the gently descending track, with a superb panorama ahead. Pass your ascent route on the right and, five minutes later (perhaps having untied and retied an animal fence across the track), *take care just in case all hell breaks loose* at the isolated farmstead on the left, **Kato Bodholakos**. The track you need to take curls left round round the farm (ignore the descending track straight ahead; it's a cul-de-sac).

Continue down the track, with lovely views opening up towards Kassiopi, below to the right. Remains of stone walls are a prominent feature in the landscape, and the hillside is a mass of flowers in the spring. Further into the descent, you look across to Albania, with its bleak and arid mountains in the distance.

About 15 minutes from the farmstead, where the track zigzags sharply to the left, a lesser track joins from the right. Turn right along this lesser track; a minute or two along, the track ends at an animal enclosure with metal fencing tied across the entrance. Do *not* go through this makeshift gate, but turn sharply left down a rather indistinct and possibly overgrown path, keeping close to a rusty metal fence on your right (which had fallen over when the walk was last checked). This path — although looking unpromising — is your way back to Imerolia.

Keep following the downhill path, which is always discernible, if somewhat overgrown in places. Soon you will see the large Kassiopi High School building below, and a concrete loading quay at the little port of Imerolia. The path now descends in zigzags, and after briefly passing through a belt of tall scrub, you emerge onto a concrete lane. Turn left to regain the main road at **Imerolia**, less than a minute below (**1h40min**). Your outgoing path is just a short way to the east. Return from here to your car or the bus shelter.

Circular walk from Acharavi

A tour leader recently sent us a description for a good circular walk of about 17km/10.5mi based on Acharavi. It will be included in a future edition of the book but in the meantime it is described in full in the Update section of our website.

Walk 3: NISSAKI • ROU • PORTA • VIGLA • KOULOURA

See map on reverse of touring map

Distance/time: 8.6km/5.4mi; 3h10min

Grade: fairly strenuous, with a steady ascent of 350m/1150ft lasting 1h15min at the start, and a steep 30-minute descent (slippery when wet) back to sea level at the end.

Equipment: boots or stout shoes with good ankle support/grip, sunhat, sunglasses, suncream, long-sleeved shirt, long trousers, fleece, raingear, swimwear, picnic, water

How to get there: 🚌 to Garnelatika, Nissaki's easternmost hamlet; alight at the gateway to the Sunshine Vacation Clubs Corfu (easily missed, but all the bus drivers know it); journey time 45min. 🚗 Parking in Nissaki is difficult. Park carefully off the side of the main road, ensuring that you do not obstruct visibility or access points.

To return: 🚌 from the Kouloura/Kalami junction, back to Corfu town (journey time 55min) or back to your car at Nissaki (15min)

Alternative walk: Nissaki — Rou — Porta — Vigla — Kouloura — Kalami — Kaminaki — Nissaki: 14.2km/8.8mi; 4h20min. Grade as main walk as far as Kouloura, then easy. Access and equipment as main walk. 🚗: *An excellent circuit for motorists.* Follow the main walk to Kouloura (3h). After a break, walk along the road round the headland to Kalami Beach. At the far end of the beach you pass the white house where Lawrence Durrell wrote *Prospero's Cell*. Follow the road up the hill, then turn left on a concrete lane and down a path, to reach the lovely cove below (Picnic 4b). From here walk along the coast, reversing the first part of Walk 4. Continue along the coast path as far as Kaminaki, then take the steep concrete road leading up to the main coast road. Either catch the bus here (to return to Corfu Town) or turn left and walk along the road back to your car in Garnelatika (15min).

This short walk, mostly well waymarked with yellow dots and arrows, makes an excellent introduction to the island. You climb high above the rocky shores of Nissaki, up through the olive groves and out into the friendly tangle of trees and bushes that patch the rugged countryside. Superb views spill out all around you. Ensconced in these declining hills is the enchanting hamlet of Rou, with its holiday homes. Descending out of these isolated hills, enigmatic Albania is tantalizingly close — just a mile and a half away, across the straits.

The walk begins across the road from the gateway to the Sunshine Vacation Clubs Corfu and a small car rental firm: climb the steps at the right of a private house. A minute uphill, just beyond an electricity pole on the left, the cobbled path rises to the right. Almost at once, head right again, crossing two water pipes. After a few metres/yards, turn left, following the cobbled path uphill, passing very close to the left-hand side of a house. Some 100m/yds further on, *take care*: turn off on a faint path to the right (it *may* be marked with yellow paint daubs).

The way climbs steadily, and the path becomes more obvious. At a fork a few minutes later, go left, up a path bordered by stone walls. Keep uphill (Picnic 3); a minute further up, by a concrete water tank, ignore the path to the right (part of the Corfu Trail). The next landmark, three minutes later, is a farm building in an olive grove off to the right, with a nearby electricity pole. Head right at the fork 40m/yds beyond the building and pole.

Meeting a TARMAC/CONCRETE ROAD (**35min**), follow it to the right uphill and rise into the hamlet of **Katavolos** by turning right, off the road (yellow waymark).

This was the charming scene which used to greet walkers entering Katavolos. Today these old pillars, no doubt built from the imitation marble quarried nearby, have been replaced by ugly concrete.

Continuing up between the houses, you catch views of Albania and Ipsos Bay, with Corfu Town behind it. The best views are still to come. Reaching the last houses, rejoin the road and follow it steadily uphill. The road reverts to concrete. In a few minutes, where the road divides, be sure take the right-hand, descending, fork. This concrete lane soon starts climbing gently, then reverts to a stone and earthen track, eventually giving superb unimpeded views across to Albania. Low grey hills roll back to a high escarpment wall of purple. Behind the hills, mirrors of blue betray the inland sea — Lake Butrinto. The only sign of civilisation comes from a patchy green plain back in the hills.

Rounding the hillside, Porta comes into sight, loosely scattered on the ridge opposite. Rou, your immediate destination, soon appears at the top of the crest not far ahead. After passing the old QUARRIES (**1h15min**) you can *either* keep ahead on this main track, bypassing Rou to the east, *or* go through Rou. If you stay on this bypass, turn off right some 50m/yds past the last houses — on an almost hidden path accompanied by a bright blue water pipe. To visit **Rou**, ascend the track to the left. Walk through the village, past a terracota-coloured house on your right*. You pass the 'Rou Estate' on your right — old village houses now converted into up-market holiday homes in traditional style. Follow steps down between renovated houses, to emerge on the bypass track you recently left. About 50m/yds past the last houses, take a path to the right. The entrance is overgrown, but follow the bright blue water pipe. This becomes a clear footpath with open views across to Albania. Emerging on a track, veer right and, where the track narrows, the footpath to Porta is on your left.

Hemmed in by thick scrub, the path dips into the gully you've been rounding. Several minutes downhill you cross a dry stream bed. Less than 10 minutes back uphill (just after crossing a water course), the path fades out, but just continue to follow the blue water pipe straight uphill, and you will soon see the path again ahead of you. Two minutes later you're in **Porta** (**1h50min**). Two cafés stand on either side of the road where you emerge, but if it's mid-afternoon, the village will be deep in slumber. (Should it be open, try the wine in the first café on your right!) Turn right and follow the road

*The owners of this house, David and Moira Baker, offer refreshments and are happy to see 'Landscapers' on their way.

through Porta. Ignore the right turn signposted to Kendroma; follow the road to the left uphill, passing a BUS SHELTER on your right. Some 250/300m/yds beyond it, as the road swings left, turn right down a concrete drive. After just 8m/yds, bear left downhill on another concreted drive (unsigned). After about 80m/yds downhill (where the concrete drive bears round to the left to a house) take the path beside a wire fence on the right. The path continues straight downhill (passing close to a chained-up dog) and emerges on a concrete lane, which you follow to the left downhill. Barely two minutes down, on a bend to the right, continue straight ahead, rejoining the path on the left.

Coming into **Vigla** (**2h05min**), join a concrete drive. Turn left downhill here, almost immediately reaching a T-junction where you turn right (near a defunct *café-neion*, now a villa). Follow the road out of the village, as it swings first to the left and then right. Then take the third concrete drive turning off to the right, following it downhill. Pass the house on the right, and continue straight down, keeping to the right of a stone wall. In spring the path may be overgrown, but it soon becomes more obvious, with the old cobblestone surface underfoot. The hillside is very steep; perfect for slipping on! Kalami Bay reappears through the olive trees, luring you down to its green and blue sea. Soon you step your way down onto a concrete drive leading to Villa Nicos. Cross the lane, with the villa's entrance gates immediately to your right, and drop steeply down a path (bearing left at the junction encountered almost immediately). Then descend a path on the right immediately beyond the swimming pool. Almost at once the path bears right, twisting down through olive trees. A few houses dot the hillside. The path drops down, with a galvanized water pipe running along the left side. Joining a concrete road, follow this downhill overlooking the romantic little cove of Kouloura, neatly tucked into the neck of a headland. Just 100m/yds downhill, turn right down a path which leads past a large building signed 'TOWN HALL' to a refreshment kiosk on the ROAD TO KASSIOPI. Turn right for 200m/yds, then head left at the KOULOURA/KALAMI JUNCTION. Three minutes along, turn left downhill on a path. It quickly leads to **Kouloura** (**3h**). After a rest and perhaps a swim, return the same way to the junction on the MAIN ROAD (**3h10min**), to catch your bus. Or continue on the Alternative walk back to Nissaki.

Walk 4: NISSAKI • KALAMI • KOULOURA • KERASIA BEACH • AG STEFANOS • KENDROMADI

See map on reverse of touring map

Distance/time: 12km/8mi; 3h50min

Grade: easy as far as Kouloura. Beyond Kouloura there are some awkward stretches, with a possibility of vertigo. The detour to the chapel of Ag Arsenious is steep and rough: care is needed. Height gain no more than 100m/330ft. Road-walking beyond Kerasia Beach.

Equipment: walking boots or stout shoes with ankle support and good grip, sunhat, sunglasses, suncream, long-sleeved shirt, long trousers, raingear, swimwear, picnic, water

How to get there: 🚍 or 🚌 to Kaminaki; alight/park carefully at the roadside at the bus stop for Kaminaki (bus journey time 45min)
To return: 🚌 from Kendromadi — back to Corfu Town (journey time 1h) or back to your car at Nissaki (journey time 15min)

Short walk: Nissaki — Kalami — Kouloura: 5.5km/3.5mi; 1h30min. Easy; access and equipment as above, but stout shoes will suffice. *I heartily recommend this for beginners.* Follow the main walk to Kouloura and from there head up to the junction on the main road for your return bus (a Kassiopi bus returning to Corfu Town or Nissaki).

Alternative walks

1 See **Alternative walk 3** on page 53.

2 **Erimiti Nature Reserve:** 8.5km/5.3mi; 2h30min. Easy; 🚌 to Kendromadi; return on 🚌 from Kassiopi. (🚍: Motorists could park at the last taverna in Ag Stefanos and start there, then take a 🚌 from Kassiopi to Kendromadi and walk from there back to their car.) Start out by leaving the bus at Kendromadi. Walk 100m/yds down the road towards Ag Stefanos, to pass the Sinies Supermarket on your left. Then fork left on the road with the 'no through road' sign and, almost immediately, take the first tarmac track on the left. Follow this to Ag Stefanos church and turn right to the sea. Just before the most northerly taverna in the village you will come to an information board ('Natural Wildlife of Erimiti') with a map on the left, detailing routes on the peninsula. (A nearby supermarket may have a guide to this small nature reserve in stock.) We've chosen to take the paths closest to the shore because the beaches are so lovely. You could just to an out-and-back or a circuit on quiet roads. Or walk on to Avlaki (where there is a good taverna) and then continue on the quiet road to Kassiopi for a bus back to Corfu Town or to Kendromadi to collect your car.

This coastal walk winds its way in and out of Corfu's most beautiful coves. The magnetic charm of these seascapes will not allow you to escape with less than a full day's rambling and swimming.

The walk starts 200m/yds east of the Shell petrol station, at the KAMINAKI BUS STOP. Take the steep concrete road leading down to the first cove, **Kaminaki** — a tourist hamlet with a touch of charm. Head left along the CORFU TRAIL, following the path up over the rocks at the end of the beach (keep to the left of the concrete platform). Within the next five minutes, you cross **Nissaki Beach** (Picnic 4a), passing in front of the NISSAKI BEACH

HOTEL. The path continues for 50m/yds above its volley ball court; ascend the steps at the centre of its grounds, almost to the front door, then head right to continue.

Rounding the hillside, and looking across the small cove shown overleaf, you'll see the inconspicuous chapel of **Ag Arsenious** set in rock ahead. Soon after spotting the chapel, fork right down a path to it. This three-minute descent is steep, slightly vertiginous and rocky, but it's a pretty spot (another setting for Picnic 4a). Swimming off the rocks here is great fun.

After your visit retrace steps to continue along the Corfu Trail which climbs some stone steps and soon turns sharp right onto a wide earth and stone track with a concrete wall on its seaward side. At a junction of tracks, head slightly uphill to the left towards another flight of stone steps. Climb these, follow a short level section of path, then drop down another flight. Having rounded this development, you now rejoin the path, still following the coast. Keep straight on to the next cove, **Agni** (**40min**). A minute along, near the end of the beach, pick up the path again, just beyond a concrete driveway. Minutes along, fork right off the main path, to follow the shore, where lovely smooth rocks slope down into the water — natural bathing platforms. You soon reach another (unnamed) beach (Picnic 4b; photograph overleaf). This one is deserted and naked of buildings — quite a surprise since, by late morning (in peak season), the horizon is dotted with boats converging on this cove-indented coastline, like a flotilla of junks seeking shelter from a typhoon.

There is a concrete shed at the point where you first come on to this deserted beach. To continue to the next 'cove of call', Lawrence Durrell's beloved Kalami, head up the dry stream bed at the right of this shed. Half a minute along, bear right, heading between fenced-in plots. Ignore the branch-off to the left a minute along; keep uphill on a concrete lane. Bear right along the lane, which soon becomes tarmac. **Kalami Beach** is just around the bend; unfortunately, an apartment complex now scars this once-idyllic little cove. The lovely large restaurant building you step past (with a terrace bar on one side) was

Looking across to the little chapel of Ag Arsenious

Durrell's home in his *Prospero's Cell* days. Take the steps down to the beach. At the end of the beach, beyond the last taverna, follow a path up to the road.

The main walk now makes for Kouloura, a little over 10 minutes away. (But between the two bays there are some exquisite swimming spots off the limestone shelves. To reach them, turn off the road about seven minutes along: the fairly steep and narrow path turns off immediately past the last house on the right.) Following the road, continue straight on at the junction, ignoring the turn-off to the left. You descend to the idyllic little harbour of **Kouloura (1h10min)**, in the shade of tall cypresses. Overlooking a small pier sheltering fishing vessels, this is probably one of the most photographed spots on the island. *(From here, those doing the Short walk should return to the junction and ascend to the main road.)*

Leaving the small harbour behind, walk back up the road for a minute and then follow the lane straight ahead and down to a quiet pebble beach, shaded by tall eucalyptus trees (Picnic 4c). Just beyond the large derelict building at the end of the beach, climb the headland. Rounding a grassy hillside, reach cove number seven — a very small, stony beach tucked into the headland opposite Kouloura. Metres along this beach, climb the hillside to rejoin your path.

The unspoilt beach just beyond Agni

About 25 minutes from Kouloura, you cross another beach — **Kerasia (1h40min)**, a large and relatively unspoilt cove, again shaded by eucalypts. Pass the taverna at the end of the beach and meet a road.* I suggest that you now turn right and *follow the road to Ag Stefanos,* rather than take the tortuous route described in the footnote which was my original route close to the coast!

The charming inlet of **Ag Stefanos (2h50min)** has become another victim of tourism, but still retains a good portion of its original rustic flavour. Leaving it behind, follow the road. Some 25 minutes uphill ignore a turning right for Avlaki. A further 35 minutes brings you to the main road at **Kendromadi (3h50min)**, where you can catch the Kassiopi bus on its way back to Nissaki and Corfu Town.

*My original route to Ag Stefanos (most users have found this too hard going): Continue past the bar, above the shore, on a good path through cypress and olive groves. It may be of interest to know that you're crossing the Rothschild property. Don't worry ... all beaches in Greece are open to the public. The turret-like construction you'll see is part of the Rothschild villa. The main path continues down to the beach, but you swing left on a lesser path, to round the point. At times rocks nosing their way out into the sea bar your way: five minutes from the last cove, where a larger outcrop of rock protrudes into the sea, climb 10m/30ft up a flight of stone steps with wooden posts for support and turn right *before* the top, looking carefully for a short, steep, overgrown and difficult path back down to the shore *(users of the Sixth edition have either not found this path or considered it too dangerous).* Then scramble along the rocky shoreline and in the water (sometimes thigh-high) until you reach the next cove. Towards the centre of the beach, an 8cm/3in black pipe runs into the sea (it is nothing more sinister than water effluent from the olive press in the village above). Alongside the pipe, the path, which is a little overgrown at the outset, eventually descends through olive groves to the tenth cove, Ag Stefanos.

Walk 5: NISSAKI • PORTA • ANO PERITHIA • LAFKI

See map on reverse of touring map

Distance/time: 16km/10mi; 5h20min

Grade: strenuous, with an overall ascent of 600m/1970ft; only recommended for experienced walkers. Snakes are not uncommon in this terrain.

Equipment: walking boots, long socks, jacket/fleece, sunhat, sunglasses, suncream, long-sleeved shirt, long trousers, raingear, picnic, plenty of water

How to get there: 🚌 to Garnelatika (as for Walk 3 on page 53); journey time 45min.

To return: 🚌 from Lafki (only one departure Mon-Sat at 15:30; recheck this departure time before setting out!)

If you're an experienced walker and don't mind crossing some rough ground, this is a fantastic hike. You cross the vast flanks of Pantokrator, where the shepherd roams with his flocks and herds of goats ... and occasionally the hunter roams with his gun. Rustic hamlets and villages lie en route; in between, rocky hillsides slide down into sheer, narrow valleys. Following the faintest of paths — and often just your nose, you trail through the loneliest landscape on the island. The countryside is undeveloped (in the best possible sense of the word) and rich in flora. With its striking panoramas, this walk lacks for nothing.

Start out by using notes for Walk 3 (page 53). Follow the route to **Porta** (**1h50min**). When you reach the road on the outskirts of Porta, where Walk 3 turns right, turn left, soon passing a large CHURCH on the right.* Three minutes above the church, turn right at a junction. Judas trees lie off the route. In spring their rich pink-to-mauve flowers hang in clusters off their leafless branches — a splendid sight. Tradition has it that this is the tree on which Judas Iscariot hung himself after denouncing Christ and, according to legend, the once-pale flowers turned pink in shame.

Mountainous Albania stretches out before you, and Lake Butrinto is visible, although partially hidden behind the coastal hills. The tiny lighthouse island of Peristator lies off Cape Varvara. Santa is the small village two ridges away. Looking up the road, you spot Mengoulas — your immediate destination. This hamlet perches high on a hillside knoll.

A good 10 minutes along the road turn left up a concrete lane into **Mengoulas**. Barely five minutes up, a

*Just 50m/yds past this church the Corfu Trail takes a woodland path to Santa before heading on to Mengoulas. You may prefer this pretty route, which adds 1km to the walk.

On the descent to Ano Perithia

Venetian manor greets you (**2h20min**). Follow the tarmac road round to the right as it passes in front of the villa, to a paved area with litter bins and a couple of mulberry trees. The road then curves round to the left and the tarmac surface reverts to a rough track; a deep ravine runs parallel to the track, on your right. Some 300m/yds along, at a T-junction with another track, turn left. At the next junction (after about 700m/yds), go straight ahead uphill. A long, steady climb up this wide track (part of the Corfu Trail) will bring you to the high pass in about 35 minutes, all the time providing you with views down over the Kerkyra Gulf and across the straits to Albania.

On the PASS (**3h**) there's a large open-sided SHELTER, where you can take a break and admire the views. *(Walk 7 joins here.)* At this stage you can also identify most of the initial descent route to Ano Perithia. Below you, to the north, you will see a shallow green valley with a few terraced fields and a low, roofless, STONE RUIN. You are aiming to walk down towards this ruin and then to pass through a steeper valley leading out of its left (western) end. Leaving the pass, take the clear path down to the left* making straight for the ruin. In the later stages of the descent there are some yellow waymarks. Some 100m/yds short of the ruin, the path turns left into a dry stream bed and merges with a path coming from the

*At press date, the Corfu Trail was still using a path about 10 minutes (700m/yds) east of the pass. This path, which leaves the main track by a large tree and a boulder marked with a yellow arrow, was quite clear initially but became very indistinct. The waymarks ran out as well. So if you use this easterly path, aim to pass to the left of the stone ruin about 10 minutes after leaving the track, then continue down the valley, heading for a narrower, V-shaped valley ahead. Cross a dry stream bed, then pick up the path again and follow the notes on page 63. This will take 15 minutes longer than the path route.

right (the Corfu Trail path at time of writing; see footnote below). Follow this steeply downhill, keeping to the left side of a steep and narrow gully. The pleasant sound of ringing bells alerts you to flocks of sheep and herds of goats, but pinpointing them amongst all this rock is another thing! Wild pears are the only trees hardy enough to survive in this rocky terrain.

Ano Perithia begins to unravel, building by building. Keep descending, wending your way between rocky outcrops. The path, not always obvious, is marked with yellow paint dots on boulders. Continue carefully down until you join a track near a WATER COLLECTION TANK. (This is the track to Lafki, which you will follow later.) Turn left on the track, and then take the next track downhill to the right, just before a CHURCH. When you reach the bottom of a flight of steps leading up to the church, fork right down a cobbled path which passes between the old village houses. In two minutes you cross a gully next to a re-roofed CHAPEL, and then briefly ascend to the main village square of **Ano Perithia** (**3h40min**; Picnic 5), where you can refuel at one of the restaurants for the final leg of the hike.

Ano Perithia was once a thriving community with grand houses and six churches. Restoration is underway,

Ano Perithia

and a new water supply has been installed. The houses are being bought and restored by the wealthy. Fortunately the village has been declared a Heritage Site by the Greek government, so all work must conform to strict regulations, maintaining its original character.

(Walk 7 leaves along the track up to the right of Taverna Capricorn; see page 75.)

After a break, head back uphill through the village to the Lafki track above the church and turn right along it. You will follow this track all the way to Lafki. From the opposite side of the valley, you have an excellent view back over Ano Perithia. Notice the interesting hill formation below the track, resembling a pack of propped-up cards.

An hour from Perithia, you round the nose of a ridge and pass above lush pastures. A large abandoned dwelling sits above the track a little further on, and a deserted hamlet hides in the trees above. A colony of beehives occupies a level field on the right of the track below the house. Soon you're overlooking an impressive valley scarred by a large quarry. Lafki lies on the far side of it. You enjoy a good coastal view of Acharavi not far below, with Roda beyond it. From the quarry, emerge on a road and turn left. In two minutes you're in **Lafki**. The BUS STOP (**5h20min**) is in the village centre.

Walk 6: NISSAKI • PALIES SINIES (PALEO CHORIO) • (MT PANTOKRATOR) • STRINILAS • EPISKEPSIS • SFAKERA • RODA

See map on reverse of touring map; see also photographs pages 2, 12, 21

Distance/time: 27km/16.7mi; 7h20min

Grade: Strenuous, with a climb and descent of about 800m/2625ft. Only fit walkers should attempt the entire hike. Most of way the hike follows tracks, but there are two short sections of pathless ascent up rocky slopes.

Equipment: walking boots, sunhat, sunglasses, suncream, long-sleeved shirt, long trousers, fleece, jacket, raingear, swimwear, picnic, water

How to get there: 🚌 to Nissaki; ask to alight at road to Viglatouri; journey time 45min.

To return: 🚌 from Roda (journey time 1h). If you cut short the hike, there are buses from Strinilas (not Sundays/holidays; journey time 1h 20min) or Episkepsis (not Sundays/holidays; journey time 1h30min).

Short walks

1 Nissaki — Palies Sinies — Nissaki: 14km/8.7mi; 3h30min. Grade: a climb and descent of 450m/1475ft, mostly on country lanes and tracks. Accesss and equipment as main walk. Follow the main walk to Palies Sinies and return the same way.

2 Strinilas — Episkepsis — Roda: 9.5km/6mi; 3h10min. A downhill walk on tracks — easy but steep and with some loose stones underfoot. Access: 🚌 Lafki bus to Strinilas; return as main walk. Follow the main walk from Strinilas (the 3h50min-point; see page 69).

Alternative walks

1 Nissaki — Palies Sinies — Ano Perithia — Loutses — Kalamaki Beach: 20km/12.4mi; 5h50min. Strenuous ascent of 680m/2230ft; only for experienced walkers. Some pathless sections both up and down steep rocky terrain. Equipment and access as main walk; return on 🚌 from Kalamaki Beach to Kassiopi, then change buses for Corfu Town (journey time 1h30min). Follow the main walk up to the pass at the 2h50min-point and turn right at the T-junction. In three minutes reach an open-sided shelter and a junction. Now follow the notes for Walk 5 from the 3h-point (page 62), to descend to Ano Perithia, then pick up Walk 7 (page 75) to go on to Kaminaki Beach.

2 Nissaki — Palies Sinies — Porta: 16km/10mi; 4h20min. Strenuous climb and descent of 680m/2230ft, but mostly along tracks. Short stretches of clambering over rocky terrain. Equipment and access as main walk; return by bus from Porta. Follow the main walk up to the pass at the 2h50min-point and turn right at the T-junction. In three minutes reach an open-sided shelter and a junction. Here turn right for Porta. At the next junction, 35 minutes later, head right — but, before you do so, continue on for another minute or so for stunning views over Porta to Albania. Just below the junction, pass a shed and take the fork to the left. Thirty minutes downhill, turn right for Porta, a good five minutes away. Pick up the bus at the turnabout/parking area in the village.

You begin this hike scaling the harsh, rock-smeared slopes of Pantokrator. On route you detour to the ruins of Palies Sinies (also known as Paleo Chorio) — a medieval village normally seen only from the summit of

Pantokrator. The greenery that envelopes it betrays its presence in this stark hilly landscape. Every crest you master reveals spectacular views. Atop Pantokrator, before gliding down to the sea, you cross a vast plateau littered with sharp rocky mounds. In springtime this great spillage of rock turns into a rock garden, as myriad flowers appear. Finally, cutting your way down through curving valleys, you make for the sea. A note of cheer returns to the landscape as you weave your way through friendly, shady olive groves and drop into a valley full of trees.

Alight from the bus at the road to Viglatouri (just two minutes past Glyfa Beach, as the bus enters **Nissaki**). Since the drivers do not know this stop, watch for the Glyfa Taverna on the right, and press the stop button on the next seaward-curving bend. **Begin the walk** by heading up the road opposite the bus stop; it is SIGN-POSTED TO VIGLATOURI, and there is a bus shelter on the right. The steep climb up this tarred road is mitigated by the wonderful views. With every turn you're overlooking the glorious Kerkyra Gulf through olive trees, with the Albanian coastline in one direction and Ipsos Bay in the other. The shimmering sea lies like a plate of glass, with not a ripple to be seen. Soon a shoulder of Pantokrator rises on the far side of a ravine; Barbati Beach lies below.

Most of the steep road up to Viglatouri is lined with beautifully sited holiday villas. About 30 minutes up from the coast road, as you enter the hamlet of **Viglatouri**, ignore a turning to the right. Keep ahead, passing VILLA ANTIGONE on the left and VILLA HELENA on the right. Five minutes uphill from this junction, after passing through olive groves and rounding a long S-bend, take a short cut: turn left on a newer tarred road, then take a steep cobbled path ascending to the right between two houses. You join a concrete drive at VILLA SIGNALO, where you continue uphill. Rejoining the tarmac road at the top of the drive, bear slightly left uphill. The road now reverts to concrete. A few minutes up, leave the olive groves behind and come onto a hillside fresh with grass. Heavy sprinklings of yellow-blooming broom lie below. Through the sheer ravine walls the coastline unravels. On fine days Corfu Town and the airport lagoon are picture-postcard clear and, beyond, the dark blue tail of the island is visible.

At a T-junction, turn left for Palies Sinies. Now, in the company of the Corfu Trail, we have to follow a road around the contours almost all the way to our destination: this fairly new road (which peters out into a track halfway round the valley) has obliterated a lovely old stone-laid path which crossed the valley sooner and saved a good 2km of contouring. But the views are superb; the radiant blue gulf, framed by the ravine walls, captures your attention.

Heading deeper into the valley, you round a bend and see the ruined buildings of an old village up ahead. Fork right on another track just below the ruins, then follow a path off the end of the track and curve round to the right

Alternative walk 2: On the descent to Porta, with Albania in the distance

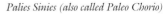
Palies Sinies (also called Paleo Chorio)

up through the ruins of **Palies Sinies** (also known as **Paleo Chorio**; **2h10min**). You pass the shell of a large old house, with a stone table outside. Where better to take a lunch break? This old village is an intriguing place to explore, but do so with the utmost care, as some of the buildings could be in a dangerous state of decay. At time of writing, however, work was going on to restore the church and its belltower. Not far past the house with the table are the old wells, on either side of the path. The water is drinkable (at time of writing they were being used by the men working on the church), but be careful when drawing it up; the well is very old and the rocks built across the top of it are not secure. (Beware also, during high summer, of hordes of wasps. Draw the water quietly.) *(Short walk 1 turns back here.)*

Leaving Palies Sinies involves a bit of scrambling; there is no path. Bear in mind that you are aiming for the track above the village. Standing between the WELLS, with your back to the village, ascend the hillside on your immediate left — making first for the church on the crest above (and slightly behind you). From the church head up the crest to the track. It's a steady climb up through the remains of terrracing and scrub.

Reaching the track, turn right and follow it for about half an hour, up to a PASS (**2h50min**). If you're not being battered by the winds, plonk yourself down and soak up this magnificent panorama. To the north, down through the V in the hills, an another almost-deserted village is visible — Ano Perithia (Walks 5 and 7), with the mountainous interior of Albania in the background.

For the main walk turn left at the T-junction here. *(But turn right for Alternative walks 1 and 2.)* Within 20 minutes you reach the road that climbs to the summit of Pantokrator. If you haven't already seen the monastery (photograph page 21), it's less than 30 minutes uphill (a detour *not* included in the overall times). Continuing to the right, you cross the plateau, weaving your way around crusty mounds of rock. Sunken, grass-lined hollows create green waterless lakes. This is goat country.

A little further on, the north coast appears, with a view over Cape Astrakeri. The return to civilisation comes when you catch sight of the small country village of Petalia below the road. Fifty minutes down from the Pantokrator junction, you emerge on another ROAD. Turn left and, five minutes later, enter **Strinilas** (**4h20min**) — by the pretty village square, shaded by a gargantuan elm tree. If you feel you've done enough today, you can catch a bus here. *(This is where Short walk 2 begins.)*

Just beyond the square, and immediately after the sign denoting the edge of the village, turn right down a concrete lane. At the T-junction 30m/yds ahead, turn left down a track (Picnic 6), which will take you to the doorstep of Episkepsis. On the way you'll spot Ag Triada, the magnificently-sited monastery visited in Walk 8, perched on the highest hill in the north. The route drops down into a concealed combe before crossing a shelf of fallow plots. Winding down through olive groves, come down onto a ROAD (**5h20min**). Turn left uphill, entering a charming archetypal farming community. Take the first turn-off right down an alley flanked by houses, to pass by the church. Keep downhill and, at the junction, descend another alley to the left, to the main road in the centre of **Episkepsis** (**5h30min**). Notice the charming three-storied Venetian manor on the right here.

Turn left on the main road; you will come to three cafés. (If you're winding up the walk here, the bus stop is 30m/yds beyond these cafés, before the sharp bend.) The final leg of the main hike begins by one of the cafés — the Ellinikon, with POST BOX outside. Head down the road alongside it, passing a church and school within a minute. Continue on through a severed arm of the village, spread along a ridge below the main village. Beyond the houses, pass a CONCRETE WELL and SHRINE and ignore a fork to the left. The lane gives way to a narrow farm track as you descend through old olive groves. About 10 minutes from the village, at a fork, ignore the track which snakes steeply downhill to the right. Climb up to the left, rounding the shoulder of a ridge, then drop down into a deep, shady valley on the far side. It's very pretty countryside; the valley floor displaying a rich assortment of foliage.

You cross a small BRIDGE and, gradually, the hills fold back to disclose a boat-shaped valley. Recross the stream

Ascending the flanks of Mt Pantokrator, you cross the plateau, weaving your way around crusty mounds of rock, where sunken grass-lined hollows create green waterless lakes.

several minutes later. A minute after this stream crossing, join a track coming from the right and follow it to the left, heading along the opposite side of the valley. Oaks make a brief appearance, then a pleasant grassy patch appears below the track. Leaving these abrupt valleys behind, your way begins opening out. A little over 10 minutes from the last stream crossing, ignore a faint track branching off to the right and, two minutes later, another track forking off right. Wending your way through the valley floor, you reach the coastal plain.

On reaching the tarmac road, turn left. In a couple of minutes, having crossed a bridge over a stream, you reach a road on the outskirts of **Sfakera** (**6h50min**). Turn right and join the main road to Roda. A further 30 minutes along this road, after crossing directly over the main coast road, will bring you to **Roda**'s beach. The BUS STOP (**7h20min**) is just where the road meets the sea — on the left side of the road, north of the crossroads.

70

Walk 7: SPARTILAS • MT PANTOKRATOR •
ANO PERITHIA • LOUTSES • KALAMAKI BEACH

See map on reverse of touring map; see also photographs pages 21, 62-63, 64 and opposite

Distance/time: 16.8km/10.5mi; 5h55min

Grade: very strenuous, with an ascent of about 600m/1970ft and descent of 906m/2970ft. For experienced walkers only. Short stretches of path are partially overgrown, and one short stretch is vertiginous. It is very rocky on top of the plateau; take your time. Do not attempt in bad weather or when there is low cloud.

Equipment: walking boots, sunhat, sunglasses, suncream, long-sleeved shirt, long trousers, raingear, swimwear, picnic, water, plenty of insect repellent in summer (when there are flies galore)

How to get there: 🚌 to Pyrgi/Ipsos (30min) and taxi from there to the village centre in Spartilas. (There is also a Spartilas bus, but it doesn't give enough time for the walk.)
To return: 🚌 from Kalamaki Beach to Kassiopi; change buses for Corfu; journey time 1h30min.

Short walk: Spartilas — Taxiarkhis Chapel — Spartilas: 3km/ 1.9mi; 1h30min. Fairly strenuous, with ascents and descents of about 280m/ 920ft; the path is partially overgrown, and there is one short vertiginous stretch. Equipment as above; access: 🚗 to/from Spartilas (park at the northern end of the village). Follow the main walk up to the chapel and return the same way.

Spend a day on the inhospitable slopes of Panto-krator — clambering up animal paths, pushing your way through scrub and floundering over rocks. No walk on the island offers so much adventure, or discomfort. For those who want the panorama without the hassles, there's a comfortable tarred road to the top. From the summit (906m/2970ft), your views stretch as far south as the islands of Paxos and Antipaxos and — on rare occasions — to the toe of Italy. What one remembers most, however, is the captivating view of neighbouring Albania. Ano Perithia, the most isolated village on Corfu, rests in a hollow of trees not far below you, girded by buffer hills of bright grey rock. This shuttered village, with its two unobtrusive restaurants, alone makes the long, arduous hike worthwhile. Our route from Spartilas to Pantokrator is also part of the Corfu Trail and well waymarked with yellow arrows.

Ask your taxi driver to drop you outside the community office (pronounced 'Kee-**no**-ti-kon gra-**fee**-on') in **Spartilas**. (If you come by bus direct to Spartilas, this office is the second stop in the village, and a sign outside reads: 'ΚΟΙΝΟΤΙΚΟΝ ΓΡΑΦΕΙΟΝ ΣΠΑΡΤΙΛΑ'.) **Start off** by heading up the right-hand alley diagonally across the road from the community office, climbing up between hillside houses. Less than half a minute up, behind the church, the path forks. Take the steps to the left. When you reach a concrete lane at the top of the steps, follow it uphill. It becomes a track. Three minutes up from the road, on a bend, leave the track and continue straight ahead on a path (the first turn-off you reach). At this stage small red and yellow dots mark your route.

The first few minutes across these hillside plots require *attention*. Pass above an uninhabited house a minute from the turn-off. When the path forks, keep left (continuing in the same direction). Then ignore a faint turn-off left. Four minutes from the track, the path abruptly swings up to the left between stone walls in varying stages of decay. It then veers back to the right again, gradually ascending above olive groves (Picnic 7) and heading along the foot of the escarpment. This much narrower path, hemmed with vegetation (including scratchy spiny broom), will remain your route all the way to the top of the plateau. There is a short stretch of vertiginous path along here.

Rounding a side-valley, you pass a ROCK (**15min**) jutting out from this scrub-covered slope; from here you have a foretaste of the panorama to come once you've reached the top. Bushes of holm oak, *Pistacia lentiscus*, spiny broom, heather and Jerusalem sage hem you in, and the path is littered with empty shotgun cartridges. Approaching the plateau, the terrain becomes rockier, pushing its way through the mat of vegetation. Clumps of heather, with purple and pink flower-heads, stand out on the hillside. Shiny-leafed strawberry trees begin appearing.

On reaching the PLATEAU (**45min**), don't miss the branch-off to the chapel of **Taxiarkhis**, barely a minute along. The path to it is over to the right and ascends through the remains of terracing. Holm oak bushes conceal the chapel, which stands just at the edge of the plateau. From here there is a spectacular panorama over the sweeping blue bays bitten out of the coastline. Stretching out before you, the island rises into a portly midriff, before tapering off into an undulating tail. And you have a bird's-eye view down onto Spartilas. Perhaps you, too, will be dismayed to find the chapel door ajar, the roof falling in, and the exquisite wall and altar frescoes left to the ravages of nature ... and man. Believe it or not, most of them are still well preserved. (*The Short walk turns back here.*)

Before heading on, verify your ongoing route from

Frescoes in the chapel of Taxiarkhis

behind the chapel. The way is through the very slight, bush-filled valley that heads directly towards Pantokrator (with the very obvious radio mast). Back on the well-marked path, keep straight ahead. Thyme and spiny broom layer the gently-subsiding inclines. Five minutes from the chapel, just after climbing the remains of a terraced embankment, the path fades. Keep straight ahead, bearing right towards the valley. A minute later, pass through an intersection, to see a STONE BUILDING (**55min**) just below the path. A path off to the right at the building takes you to a beautiful stone-laid WHEAT THRESHING FLOOR hidden in the trees. It's a very pretty spot. Ignore all the paths striking off uphill and out of the valley. Your way burrows through the scrub lining the V in the slope. At intervals, terraced plots appear through the bushes on the right. In summer this shady path which tunnels its way through holm oaks, provides a welcome break from the hot sun; in spring moss cushions the rock.

About 10 minutes from the stone building, you leave the oak forest. The path becomes rougher and enters a gully. Continue up the floor of the gully. When you notice a track above you, scramble over the boulders to reach it. Go left, but then immediately leave the track on the outside of a sharp bend. (If you scrambled up and joined the track a little further west, turn *right* on the track and then turn left on the outside of the same sharp bend.) The footpath you now follow is a continuation of the gully. Grazing animals have made several paths in this area; keep to the main path, climbing up small terraces.

Five minutes above the track, you reach another, higher level in the plateau. A grass-covered plain leads up to a choppy sea of rocky hummocks rising and falling all round. Beyond this unruliness lies Mt Pantokrator. Follow the waymarking: in summer, within seconds of entering the dry grass, flies will descend on you by the thousands, trying to crawl into every orifice laid open to them. Don't even cough, it's too risky! The bright side of this onslaught is that — tired though you may be — you certainly quicken your pace! *(If at this stage cloud or bad weather threaten, do not attempt to go further!)*

A couple of minutes across this extensive flat area swing left, following a slight depression. You briefly leave the grassy plots and head across a rock-strewn plain. Then the way becomes like an obstacle course, as you climb in and out of sunken pastures amidst this mass of rock. *Keep your eye on the waymarking*; it's easy to head off in the wrong direction! *Ignore* all the lettering waymarks; *follow* the arrows and dots. Small, long-stemmed *Euphorbia myrsinites* grows up here amidst the rock, and in autumn golden-headed thistles *(Pallenis spinosa)* cover the rocky slopes. Closer to Pantokrator the mounds become sharper and the hollows deeper.

Crossing a crest, the mountain road comes into sight. From here on the waymarking is faded and infrequent. If you lose the trail, just make for the road. Descending, remains of an old path appear. Dip down into a large valley cutting across in front of you. Bear left along it and, when you reach a double terraced wall, pick up a clear path ascending to the Pantokrator road, opposite a large CONCRETE WATER TANK (**2h**).

Turn right, making for the summit and the monastery, passing a pretty shaded hillside hollow. A little further on, you're overlooking Ano Perithia, a haven of greenery, swallowed up by a mass of tumbling, rocky slopes — a welcoming sight in this bleak landscape. Passing under the belfry, you enter the grounds of **Moni Pantokrator** (**2h25min**). The towering radio mast certainly doesn't help this already-naked enclosure. The back of the building, with its cloister arches, is more appealing (photograph page 21). There are some faded 17th-century frescoes in the chapel.

Descend the road from the monastery and take the first track turning off to the right. Follow this track for the next 20 minutes, descending gently, and pass a large LIVESTOCK SHED, just below the track on your left (**3h**).

Continue along the track, soon ignoring another track on the right (which leads to Palies Sinies on the Walk 6 ascent route). You soon arrive at an open-sided SHELTER, from where you can admire the fantastic views both to the north and south.

Now use the notes for Walk 5 on page 62 from the 3h-point, to reach **Ano Perithia (3h55min)**.

Leaving Ano Perithia, head up to the right of Taverna Capricorn, between more shuttered houses. Tall, yellow-flowering stems of mullein line the roadside. Follow this road all the way to **Loutses (4h35min)**, which appears before a stunning backdrop of glimmering sea and the enormous shadowy mountains of Albania. (If you're catching a bus here, *ignore* the first bus stop (it's no longer used as a bus stop); go on to a second bus stop less than 15 minutes further on, where you can wait in the comfort of a café.)

Those bound for Kalamaki Beach, however, turn up the first road branching off right, five minutes below the first bus stop/turnabout. Pass through a small cluster of houses, keeping right at the first fork (a minute along), and left at the second (three minutes later), following the tarmac road. At the end of the road lies the tiny village of **Anapaftiria (4h55min)**. From here follow the wide farm track that continues on past the houses. Two minutes down, you're looking across the cerulean sea to Albania. This marvellous view remains with you for the rest of the hike. The track zigzags lazily down to the sea. There are no turn-offs. Sea squill, a lovely sight with its flowering white stem, is sprinkled liberally across the hillside. Nearing the sea, *Cardopatium corymbosum* — a tall thistle with clustered flowerheads — competes with mullein stalks for height.

Sandy Kalamaki Beach appears over to the left. Soon after, the track enters a scattering of bushes and laurels. Ignore a track off left. Fifty minutes downhill you meet the road, just above **Seki Bay (5h45min)**, a pretty little cove concealed by cypress trees. There is a small taverna (not always open, unfortunately) on the main road. If you stop here, allow at least 10 minutes to reach your bus shelter. It's along to the left, before **Kalamaki Beach (5h55min)**.

Walk 8: NIMFES • MONI AG TRIADA • KLIMATIA

See map on reverse of touring map

Distance/time: 13km/8mi; 3h55min

Grade: moderate, with a steep descent of 100m/330ft to the valley floor (extra care needed when wet), followed by an ascent of 350m/1150ft to Moni Ag Triada. At times the stream is too full to cross, and you will have to retrace your steps to Nimfes to continue the walk.

Equipment: walking boots or stout shoes, sunhat, sunglasses, sun-cream, long-sleeved shirt, long trousers, raingear, picnic, water

How to get there: Roda 🚌 to the Nimfes turn-off about 2km beyond Ag Douli; journey time 50min

To return: 🚌 from Klimatia (*not in the timetables;* departs Mon-Sat at 15.00 only)

Short walk: Nimfes — Moni Pantokrator of Nimfes — Nimfes: 5.5km/3.5mi: 2h05min. Easy; stout shoes will suffice. 🚌 as above, or 🚗 to/from Nimfes: park in the wide street near the fountain and public garden, shortening the walk by 1h10min. Follow the main walk until it turns off to Ag Triada (at the 1h20min-point). Here keep right, to return to Nimfes (1h30min), then descend to the bus stop (2h05min).

Alternative walks

1 Nimfes — Moni Ag Triada — Klimatia: 8.5km/ 5.3mi; 2h45min. Moderate, with a steepish climb of about 275m/900ft to the monastery. Transport as main walk. From the fountain in Nimfes, cross the road and continue up the road branching off almost opposite the fountain. A little over five minutes along, you join the main walk at the 1h20min-point. Pick up the notes opposite.

2 Nimfes — Moni Pantokrator — Moni Ag Triada — Klimatia — Nimfes: 17km/10.5mi; 4h55min. Grade as main walk as far as Klimatia, then easy road-walking back to Nimfes. Follow the main walk to the 3h55min-point, then turn right and follow the road back to Nimfes (about 4km; 1h).

This walk calls at two of the island's little-visited *monis,* each in a different setting. Moni Pantokrator of Nimfes sits concealed in a hillside cypress wood, high above a lush valley. Moni Ag Triada adorns a cone-shaped hill with a wonderful view across the olive-studded north. You head from a luxuriant valley full of gardens and trees up to the drier, stonier, olive-clad slopes. Climbing to the summit of a rocky peak, you're surrounded by soft pink heather and shiny-leafed straw-berry trees. Descending back into the olive groves, you pass one of the island's few remaining holm oak boskets.

Start out at the NIMFES JUNCTION on the Roda road. Head straight up to **Nimfes (35min)**. This village, a kind combination of new and old, sprawls across a ridge. Keep right at the fork by a memorial and a church. A few minutes further on, the sound of gushing water announces a nine-spouted fountain below the road. The turn-off for Moni Pantokrator of Nimfes lies 40m/yds further on, just past the public garden. Branch off right on a wide concrete lane. Two minutes up, at the top of a rise, head right along a concrete track into olive groves. Ignore the lane off right a minute along and a track off left minutes later. About 15 minutes from Nimfes you come to a chapel with a sprinkling of chestnut trees around it. Take the path to the right of the chapel; a minute downhill, you're at the abandoned monastery **Pantokrator of Nimfes** (**55min**; Picnic 8).

Descend the steps leading out of the grounds; you come to a spring a minute below. Scramble up behind the spring and have a look at the tiny CAVE CHAPEL. Descending into the valley, the way passes the spring, curves to the right, then drops to the left. Reaching the flat along the stream, you cross a track, and then the way swings right to cross the stream. The log bridge at the crossing point is often swept away, and if the stream is in spate, you may have to retrace your steps to Nimfes to continue the walk — although most readers are finding crossing points upstream or down! If you *can* cross, rise to the farm track on the far side and turn right. About 15 minutes along the track, at a junction, keep right. Ignore two turn-offs to the left, cross a concrete bridge, and pass a concrete block shed on the right. Stay on the main track.

Coming out on the NIMFES ROAD (**1h20min**), head left for Agia Triada. *(Here the Short walk turns right, back to Nimfes, and the Alternative walk joins the main walk.)*

Moni Pantokrator of Nimfes (Picnic 8)

Almost at once, pass the football pitch and continue ahead, ignoring the concrete track rising to the right. The valley continues on towards the bulky mass of Pantokrator. Just over five minutes along, the way forks. Go right, climbing the slope. Another steep ascent lies before you, up a rough gravel track. The hillside below is like an arboretum. A tiny spring sits on the right some minutes uphill; across the way there's a water catchment tank.

Stay on the main track. Ignore tracks joining from either side and keep going along the track until, around 50 minutes uphill, you meet a junction where you turn right. From here the chapel is visible on the summit. The track passes through olive groves and shortly emerges into hillside scrub. Ahead you will see a raw track scarring the hillside below the chapel. Follow this track uphill as it winds its way around the shoulder of the hill until you reach a concrete driveway. Turn right and follow this up to the hilltop, crowned by **Moni Ag Triada** (**2h50min**). From here you overlook the long, gently curving bay at Roda. Near the chapel there are seats for a relaxing break or perhaps a picnic, and three friendly dogs to keep you company.

Leaving, return on the same track, following it all the way to Klimatia. The Theapondinisi Islands come into sight, barely visible in a summer haze. A little over 10 minutes down, ignore a track turning off to the right and, 10 minutes later, ignore a fork to the left. Coming into the outskirts of **Klimatia**, you meet the road just by the BUS STOP (**3h55min**). If you've missed the three o'clock bus, walk on to the main Roda/Corfu road, 40 minutes away, for the Roda/Corfu bus.

Walk 9: small lake and vineyards on the way to Spartilas

Walk 9: TROUMPETA • SOKRAKI • SPARTILAS • (PYRGI)

See map on reverse of touring map; see photograph opposite

Distance/time: 11.3km/7mi; 2h55min

Grade: easy walking on roads and tracks, with just one short stretch on slightly overgrown paths; initial ascent of 175m/560ft

Equipment: walking boots or stout shoes with ankle support, sunhat, sunglasses, suncream, long-sleeved shirt, long trousers, picnic, water, swimwear (if going on to Pyrgi), fleece, raingear

How to get there: 🚌 (Roda or Sidari bus) to Troumpeta; journey time 35min

To return: 🚌 from Spartilas (journey time 40min) or Pyrgi/Ipsos (journey time 25min)

Short walks

1 Troumpeta to Sokraki: 5.8km/3.6mi; 1h15min. Easy, but initial ascent of 175m/560ft; all along a road; equipment and access as main walk; return by 🚌 from Sokraki. Follow the main walk to Sokraki.

2 Sokraki to Spartilas: 5.3km/3.3mi; 1h45min. Grade and equipment as main walk. Only one suitable outgoing bus a day to Sokraki, at 14.00 (not Sundays/holidays). Follow the main walk from Sokraki (the 1h10min-point); return by bus as main walk.

3 Circuit from Sokraki: 5.8km/3.6mi; 2h20min. Grade and equipment as main walk. Especially recommended for motorists. 🚌 or 🚗 to Sokraki; park by the side of the road as you leave Sokraki for Zigos. Follow the main walk from the 1h10min-point to the 2h15min-point. Then turn right along the track and, after several minutes, at a fork, bear right uphill. Keep on this track, ignoring side-turnings. As you ascend the hillside, the views to the east and south are superb, the islands of Lazareto and Vido being clearly visible, as well as Corfu Town, the Halkiopoulos Lagoon and the hills beyond. Keep following the track until it bends sharply round to the right and crosses a small plateau, where you rejoin your outward track. Turn left and within 10 minutes you are back on the edge of Sokraki.

This walk follows the spine of an abrupt escarpment wall stretching from east to west, severing the head of the island. The views are fine, stretching both northward and to the south — from subdued rolling countryside to a bright, curvaceous coastline. This is rural Corfu at its best, despite the asphalting of the old track from Troumpeta to Sokraki (there's very little traffic on the road, and it's below the tourist radar in any case).

Start off in the hamlet of **Troumpeta**, just at the top of the pass (where the bus stops). Head back south along the road towards Corfu Town. Some 50m/yds downhill, fork left on an asphalt road climbing the face of the escarpment. This road, which does not see much traffic, will take you all the way to Sokraki. Early on in the climb, you're overlooking the central lowlands and, further east, the noticeable hayfields of the Ropa Plain. Liapades, over to the right, is the first village to appear.

Shortly after, Doukades creeps into sight. Some **15min** uphill, the panorama extends to the north (Picnic 9). On a clear day you can see the Theapondinisi Islands: Othoni (the largest), Erikoussa (over to the right) and Sanothraki — all inhabited but untouched by tourism, save for one small hotel on Erikoussa. (The islands can be reached daily from Corfu Town by slow ferry or more quickly by ferry from Ag Stefanos in the west.)

Heading up the spine of the ridge, you come upon fallow plots. Approaching the **30min**-mark, come alongside a small flat area with a few surrounding terraces. The crest is speckled with rock, which turns to a burning white under the relentless midday sun. The remains of a homestead sit on the edge of the flat area, almost obscured by trees and holly oak bushes. Closer to the road there's a WELL, but the water is only fit for animals.

Continuing towards Sokraki, pass by orchards, vineyards, and small gardens — all with backdrops of maquis. Cypress trees dot the hillsides. You pass a track branching off left (**40min**). Two minutes later, some farm dwellings appear on a wooded hillock above the road. Just around the bend, the bold mound of Pantokrator fills the view. Villagers may pass by: in the old days they would be accompanied by laden donkeys, with a goat or two wandering along in front, and a dog trailing far behind. Nowadays, they hurtle by in pick-ups. Shortly after passing a track forking off left, you round a bend and look across a cultivated basin to Sokraki. Entering the village, you snatch a view of the gulf. Ignore a minor road and a wider road off to the right; bear left along the road through the centre of **Sokraki** (**1h10min**), passing a number of cafés. *(Short walk 1 ends here; Short walks 2 and 3 begin here.)*

The ongoing walk to Spartilas now follows part of the Corfu Trail and is waymarked with yellow arrows and dots. Ignore the road turning off to the right; leave Sokraki on the main road. On a bend just outside the village, some metres past the 'Sokraki' sign, fork right on a track, to return to the crest of the ridge. Within 10 minutes you're above a cascade of fallow terraced plots running down the valley floor. A little further on, the track forks: keep left (more or less straight ahead; *the track to the right is the return route for Short walk 3*). Soon the mass of Pantokrator appears (try to ignore the rubbish tips to the left of the track). Sgourades is seen across the valley. The track descends to a CLEARING. Fork right to leave the clearing on a lovely woodland path and descend to the valley floor. Minutes from the clearing, you pass between terraced fields amidst the scrub. Keep to the main path as it bears right here, but ignore all faint paths off to the right.

The path is interrupted by a crossing BULLDOZED TRACK, but continues on the far side — alongside another bulldozed track. *Keep to the path or it will disappear!* Path and track converge at a STONE HUT, then the path continues separately. The clear path bears slightly right, as you descend through overgrown and abandoned plots, hemmed in by trees and bushes. Some of the terraces you clamber down while following this beautiful, wooded path are quite high. When you meet the track again, follow it for just 50m/yds, then pick up your path again, on the left. Emerging from the scrub, you come into farmland — olive groves, fruit trees, vegetable plots, and vineyards. The way now heads across the right-hand side of the valley. A minute along, you come to a concrete wall below a vineyard, on the far side of which stands a pergola. Swing right in front of the wall, to reach a TRACK just above (**2h15min**). Turn left on the track (*Short walk 3 turns right*). The track soon becomes a tarmac country road and takes you to Spartilas, passing carefully tended vineyards and a small lake full of noisy toads on your left.

Follow the road to a junction, where you turn right. A minute downhill, you have an excellent view of Spartilas from a parking area on the right. **Spartilas** (**2h55min**) is set in a crease in the mountain wall, with a superb outlook over the gulf. The BUS STOP (unmarked) is just past the community office ('ΚΟΙΝΟΤΙΚΟΝ ΓΡΑΦΕΙΟΝ ΣΠΑΡΤΙΛΑ') on your right.

But if you still have some bounce left in you, why not walk on to Pyrgi, just over an hour away? The route alternates between road and cobbled path and is a pleasant descent if there isn't too much traffic. To get there, turn right downhill on the alley just before the community office. Fork left at the back of the building and then keep down to the right. Two minutes from the road, when the way becomes a wide lane, take the wide steps down to the right. Continue down the steps until you reach the road. Now keep descending on the short-cut path, cutting loops off the road. The last piece of path takes you down to the road at the sea front in Pyrgi, by the bus stop (1h05min from Spartilas).

Walk 10: PEROULADES • CAPE DRASTIS • PEROULADES • AVLIOTES • MAGOULADES

Distance/time: 12km/7.5mi; 3h55min

Grade: easy to moderate; overall climbs totalling about 200m/650ft, with one fairly steep ascent of about 80m/260ft, lasting 10 minutes. The track to Cape Drastis may be unpleasantly trafficked in summer.

Equipment: walking boots or shoes with good grip, sunhat, sunglasses, suncream, long-sleeved shirt, long trousers, fleece, raingear, swimwear, picnic, water

How to get there: 🚌 to Peroulades; journey time 1h20min
To return: 🚌 from Magoulades; journey time 1h10min

Short walks

1 **Peroulades — Cape Drastis — Peroulades:** 2.8km/1.8mi; 1h10min. Grade and equipment as above; 🚌 or 🚗 to/from Peroulades (park in the village square). Include the local beach as well and make it a 'beach day'. Follow the main walk to the cape and back.

2 **Magoulades — Moni Ipsili and Moni Ithamini — Magoulades:** 6.5km/4mi; 1h40min. Easy; stout shoes will suffice. 🚗 to/from Magoulades (bus times are inconvenient); park near the church at the top of the village. Follow the road opposite the church, walking all the way along the top of the ridge. In 30min join a track coming from the left. In less than a minute you are at the junction for the monasteries. Pick up the main walk at the 2h50min-point and follow it to the end.

The magnificent bluffs of Cape Drastis will take your breath away. Minuscule off-shore islands, finely etched with circles, look fresh off a potters' wheel. A tiny cove, set deep in the cliff-hanging cape, is a peaceful bathing spot outside high season. (The sandy village beach at the foot of high cliffs is just as impressive, but usually more crowded.) Later in the walk, you head into the quiet inland hills, under the shade of the ubiquitous olive tree, to the walled-in silence of two monasteries. Motorists may prefer to do the two Short walks individually, to avoid the longish stretch of road-walking linking the beauty spots of Drastis and the monasteries.

The walk begins at the parking area/bus stop just

Moni Ipsili

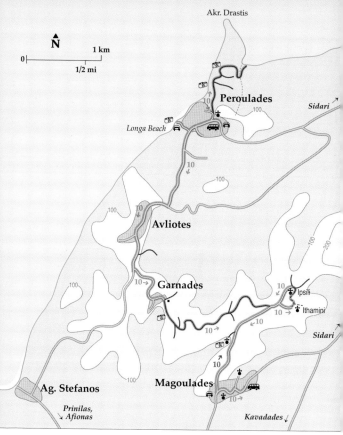

below the village square in **Peroulades**. Walk some 30m/yds along the main road further into the village. Then turn right up a concrete lane signposted 'CAPE DRASTIS'. Head up to the church and school (in the same grounds), then keep straight uphill, climbing a motorable track past the left-hand side of the school. Keeping to this main track, cross the brow of the hill and begin descending. There may be signs urging you down to 'Beach', and in high season you will encounter traffic here, although outside July and August there should only be a trickle. Albania, stretching across the horizon in front of you, is a continuous line of mountains.

Some 50m/yds downhill, climb up left to a viewpoint, but be very *careful* here: without warning, you'll find yourself on the edge of a precipice, where dazzling, pearl-white cliffs slice their way around the point. Past the viewpoint, ignore the track heading inland; keep straight on. The view par excellence over this beauty spot, shown on page 85, unfolds three minutes later. You look out over an arc of islets just off-shore. The COVE at **Cape**

*Left: Sunset Beach at Peroulades;
right: the 'view par excellence' over
Cape Drastis*

Drastis (**30min**) is an excellent swimming spot, as it is not too deep and it's easy to scramble out of the water. The backdrop is an impressive white wall rising straight up out of a crystal-blue sea. In high season there are likely to be a few fellows here renting umbrellas and sunbeds and selling cold drinks.

Return to **Peroulades** (**1h05min**) on the same track and turn right below the school, along the village road. Three minutes along, take the first tarred lane branching off to the right, signposted 'LOGAS BEACH/TAVERNA SUNSET'. Barely a minute along, turn right again, passing the restaurant on the right, and continue for 200m/yds to a parking area on the clifftop. Just below you (but still out of sight) stretches the spectacular beach shown above. Only a collar of sand separates the sea from the base of the high cliffs. A steep path plonks you down onto the beach in two minutes.

Return from the beach to the turn-off and head right towards Avliotes, following a winding country road between fields. At the junction, a good five minutes along, fork right (to continue more or less straight ahead). Some 25 minutes from the beach, meet the main road and head uphill to the right, through **Avliotes** (**1h40min**). A good five minutes sees you at the far end of this unprepossessing village where, at a junction, you head left towards Ag Stefanos (signposted).

Ignore the first turn-off to the left but, 10 minutes from Avliotes, turn off left onto an unsigned tarmac road (the second left turn you come to). The road climbs towards Garnades. After a steep uphill section, ignore the turning to the right and continue ahead. *Zorro* — masked sheep with uneven black socks — sometimes graze the inclines here. When the tarred road ends, at a pink house, continue on a track striking uphill to the right. Shortly, Cape Arilas and Gravia Island appear through an open V in the hills to your right. Keep straight ahead along the

track. Soon you have views to the left to Avliotes, a blend of pinkish buildings stepping the crest of a ridge on the far side of the valley. It looks more attractive when seen from afar.

Half an hour up from the road junction (10 minutes from Avliotes) you reach a four-way junction of tracks. Keep straight ahead uphill along a widened track lightly sprayed with tar. A little over five minutes uphill from the junction join a tarmac road. Follow it to the left for two minutes, then take the tarmac drive off right down to **Moni Ithamini** (3h), snuggled into a hillside hollow under citrus trees, loquats and elms. The monastery building is now a European Youth Centre.

From Moni Ithamini take the path around the left of the building, then follow a track uphill, round the shoulder of the hill. The next monastery is hidden among the trees above you on the left. Turn left at the next junction and follow a concrete lane up to **Moni Ipsili** (3h05min), which boasts some valuable icons and paintings (but they are kept locked away).

To continue the walk, descend the concrete lane to the road and follow it to the left. No turn-offs are required, but you might like to detour to an isolated church up on your right some 10 minutes along, to enjoy the views. Continue along the road and descend into **Magoulades**. A church stands opposite the road junction. Turn left and pass through this very colourful village. Less than 20 minutes downhill come to the BUS STOP (3h55min) for buses to Corfu Town.

Walk 11: PALEOKASTRITSA • LAKONES • MAKRADES • AG GEORGIOS BAY • AFIONAS • PORT TIMONE • AFIONAS

See map page 90-91; see photographs pages 10-11, 28

Distance/time: 17.2km/10.8mi; 4h55min

Grade: strenuous, with overall ascents/descents of 500m/1650ft. The paths are slippery in wet weather.

Equipment: walking boots or stout shoes with good grip and ankle support, sunhat, sunglasses, suncream, long-sleeved shirt, fleece, long trousers, rainwear, swimwear, picnic, water

How to get there: 🚌 to Paleokastritsa (journey time 40min)
To return: 🚌 from Afionas; journey time 2h15min. The departure time of this bus varies, so it is best to arrive early! Or, when you reach Afionas, telephone at one of the cafés for a Sidari taxi, to take you to Sidari, for better bus connections.

Short walks

1 Afionas — Port Timone — Afionas: 2km/1.3mi; 1h10min. Moderate descent/ascent of 100m/330ft; wear stout shoes. 🚌 to and from Afionas; park in the village, at the end of the road, keeping well clear of the square where the bus turns round. Pick up the main walk at the 3h45min-point and follow it to the end.

2 Afionas — Cape Arilla — Afionas: 1km/0.7mi; 30min. Easy; access as Short walk (1) above. Pick up the main walk at the 4h55min-point and follow it to the viewpoint (Picnic 11b) and back to the village.

Alternative walk: Ag Georgios — Afionas — Port Timone — Afionas — Ag Georgios: 8km/5mi; 2h40min. Moderate, with overall descents/ ascents of 400m/1300ft; equipment as main walk. This is a pleasant 'out and back' walk most suitable for motorists; leave your 🚗 at the long sandy beach of Ag. Georgios. This is the 2h50min-point in the main walk: follow the notes on page 89 all the way to Afionas. Then retrace your outward route back down to Ag Georgios, where you can swim again or have some refreshments.

Paleokastritsa is Corfu's tourist mecca. But, fortunately, tourist development has not yet disfigured this natural asset. This walk is all about wonderful views. After the initial steep climb up to the hill village of Lakones, your first views are back down to the pine-fringed beaches around Paleokastritsa. Still climbing, the walk heads inland to the attractive village of Makrades and, soon afterwards, as you descend an old zigzag mule trail, there are more glorious views over the shimmering horseshoe bay of Ag Georgios. After a longish stretch along the sandy beach, the path again climbs to the hilltop village of Afionas, with the final part of the walk (an 'out and back route') providing yet more fine views over the twin coves of Port Timone.

The walk begins at the CAR PARK/BUS TERMINUS in **Paleokastritsa**. Walk back along the main road for about 200m/yds. Then take the first turn-off left, just beyond another parking area and opposite the SUPERMARKET KATHY. Some 70m/yds uphill, go right at a fork. This is where the real ascent begins. Continue up this road for about 10 minutes (just under 400m/yds), to a point where the road flattens out. Turn left here on a track. Soon the track forks; keep right here (signposted). After about 100m/yds you're on a lovely old stone-paved path. A few minutes up, a path joins from the right; keep straight on, under the shade of olive trees. Half-moons of terracing stretch across the hillside.

Midway up to Lakones, you enter a passageway slicing up through a vertical rock face. Out of the passage and back into terraced hillsides, you cross a track, and then enter **Lakones**. The path veers right, to where an alley cuts across in front of you. Turn left up the alley and, on meeting the ROAD (**40min**), turn left. *(Walk 12 turns right here.)*

Walk along the narrow street, watching out for traffic which is one-way and controlled by lights at each end of the village. As the buildings start to thin out, there are fine views down to the coast below. Five minutes along, leave the road, climbing steps up to a path opposite a shop (ALKI'S ARTIST OLIVE WOOD PRODUCTION). A little over 10 minutes up, a steel frame (the remains of a greenhouse) is visible across the valley floor on the left. Ignoring any side paths to the right or left, keep to the main path (although it may be narrow and edged with prickly plants at first). When you are directly across the valley from the framework, continue along the main path: it widens out and after about 100m/yds bends left, rounds the head of the shallow valley and comes to a

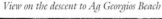

View on the descent to Ag Georgios Beach

Left: the old mule trail down to Ag Georgios Beach; right: Afionas

T-junction, where you turn right. Quickly reaching the MAIN ROAD, turn left (**1h05min**).

Follow the road to the outskirts of Vistonas. Just past the **Vistonas** sign, turn left on a concrete lane (beside a SHRINE at the side of the road). It takes you past a church. From the church keep straight downhill on a path through olive trees, rejoining the road after 200m/yds. On coming to the MAKRADES JUNCTION (**1h25min**), make a dash to the right, before the stall-keepers rush out to insist you taste their local wines from the barrel!* Continue through **Makrades** until, just past the last houses and a cafeneion, you come to a lane cutting across in front of you (concrete to the right and tarmac to the left). Head right along the concrete lane. A few minutes down, a neat concreted path, bordered by low stone walls, joins the track from the left. (*This is where Walk 12 turns left to Krini, another pretty hilltop village.*)

Ten minutes downhill, the track comes to a dead end at a barrier for vehicles. Ahead lies the most unexpected sight: a path — the old mule 'road' down to the sea — cuts through a corridor in the hillside rock. Once through it, you're virtually 'hanging' out over glorious Ag Georgiou Bay; the piercing blue sea, trimmed in turquoise, shimmers below. Clinging to the escarpment, this old mule road descends in zigzags, with views across the translucent bay to Cape Arilla and the Thea-pondinisi Islands. Ten minutes down, when you join a track, turn left downhill, towards the coast. At the junction that follows, bear right along a track running parallel with the bay. This is a beautiful stroll, looking through the olive trees down onto the green sea. Various

*A user writes amusingly 'The wine-sellers at the Makrades junction have clearly been reading *Landscapes of Corfu*, for they will now be waiting for you well before the turn-off. Beware, these little old ladies think nothing of jumping out in front of moving cars, so mere walkers are easy targets for them!'

tracks lead down to the sea; you could explore any one of them. About 50 minutes after leaving the zigzag mule path, you reach **Ag Georgios Beach** (**2h 50min**; Picnic 11a).

Walk along the track behind the beach, and you will come to the RESORT of **Ag Georgios** in about 10 minutes. This settlement is not based around a village, but has grown up as a result of the popularity of its 3km-long sandy beach. The resort is divided into three sections because there is no coastal road all along the seafront. Having perhaps stopped for a swim or refreshment, continue to the far end of the beach and walk over towards the road that ascends to Afionas. A steep 15-minute climb takes you up to a T-junction; turn left. Ten minutes later you're in the square at **Afionas** (**3h45min**). Its strategic setting makes Afionas prone to winds, but the villagers must think the views compensate for the inconvenience.

Now make for Cape Arilla: standing with your back to the church door, head off into the alley 10m/yds to the left. (by the sign for 'DIONYSOS TAVERNA'). After 70m/yds, turn left on a path. If you want to head for the little beaches at Port Timone or walk on to the *moni* beyond them, take the path which then drops downhill to the left. If you prefer to make for the VIEWPOINT overlooking these coves, keep up at a higher level, turning right on a path with a fence on the right. This path, though not always immediately obvious, is well defined. The views from this side of Ag Georgios are as appealing as those enjoyed earlier. The crystal-clear sea is almost hypnotic. Rounding the hillside, the two bright little coves shown on pages 10-11 shine up at you (Picnic 11b). In ancient times the larger cove was known as the Tiller's Port (**Port Timone**; **4h15min**), where boats came to shelter from approaching storms. A collar of land separates the two. The promontory joined to this tiny necklace of land is tightly woven in maquis. Three trails with colour-coded signposts lead off from the viewpoint — to the headland *moni* and the beaches.

Back at the square in **Afionas** (**4h55min**), be sure to take the wide alley uphill, opposite the church, to climb to the spine of the ridge, with great views northwards over Arilla Bay (see notes for Picnic 11b on page 11).

Walk 12: PALEOKASTRITSA • LAKONES • MT ARAKLI • MAKRADES • KRINI • ANGELOKASTRO • PALEOKASTRITSA

See also photographs page 18-19, 31

Distance/time: 11.4km/7.1mi; 4h

Grade: moderate-strenuous, with an initial ascent of 450m/1500ft and a descent of 300m/1000ft at the end. Some of the paths can be slippery when wet; possibility of vertigo at Angelokastro

Equipment: walking boots, sunhat, suncream, sunglasses, long-sleeved shirt, raingear, picnic, water

How to get there and return: 🚌 (journey time 40min) or 🚗 to/from Paleokastritsa; park in the car park below the monastery

Short walks (access and equipment as main walk)

1 Paleokastritsa — Lakones — Mt Arakli (obelisk) — Paleokastritsa: 5km/3mi; 2h30min. Moderate-strenuous; overall ascent/descent of 450m/1500ft. Follow the main walk as far as the obelisk on the east flank of Mt Arakli (1h20min), then return the same way.

2 Paleokastritsa — Lakones — Paleokastritsa: 2.5km/1.5mi; 1h30min. Moderate; overall ascent/descent of 275m/900ft (the ascent to Lakones is steep). Follow the main walk up to Lakones and, when you reach the main road in the village, turn left. Walk along through the village until you reach Alki's Artist Olive Wood Production. Turn down the steps at the far side of this shop and follow the main walk from the 3h15-point (page 93) back down to Paleokastritsa.

3 Paleokastritsa — Lakones — Angelokastro — Paleokastritsa: 7.8km/4.9mi; 3h10min. Moderate-strenuous; overall ascent/descent of 330m/1075ft (the ascent to Lakones and the castle is steep). This is a popular route with 'Landscapers'. Follow the main walk up to Lakones and from there walk along the road through the village towards Krini. Continue past Bella Vista ('the best view in Europe') and a couple of restaurants with tables overlooking the turquoise coastline. Follow the road for 2.3km/1.4mi, and pass a convent on the left. On a long stretch of straight road, take a path on the left indicated by a yellow Corfu Trail marker. This descends into an olive grove and then a stream bed. After a few metres, leave the stream bed by taking a path to the right. Bear right and follow the path ahead, through the trees. It soon becomes a track and climbs. On a bend, take a path (by a rock), climbing gently to the main village road on the edge of Krini. Turn left here and follow the road downhill for 10 minutes, to Angelokastro. On the return leg, you could divert into Krini or visit the old threshing floor (Picnic 12b), before heading back to Lakones and Paleokastritsa.

It's hard to imagine Paleokastritsa as a humble fishing village before the onset of tourism. Set amid a sequence of turquoise bays and rocky coves, backed by tumbling green hillsides and the dominant bulk of Mt Arakli, it must have been incomparably beautiful. Although tourist development has taken a definite toll, the natural beauty of the landscape can perhaps be best appreciated by venturing into the mountainous hinterland, with numerous viewpoints over the dramatic coastline. This walk makes a circuit up the flanks of Mt Arakli, giving unsurpassed views of the Bay of Liapades. It follows old stone-paved paths and donkey tracks, visiting three attractive hillside villages on the way and then, returning towards the coast, it leads you to a steep climb up to the rocky fortress of Angelokastro. The few skeletal remains have little to offer, but its sheer-sided perch will leave you in awe — if not fright — as you peer down into a milky-green sea 330m/1075ft below.

Begin the walk by following the notes for WALK 11

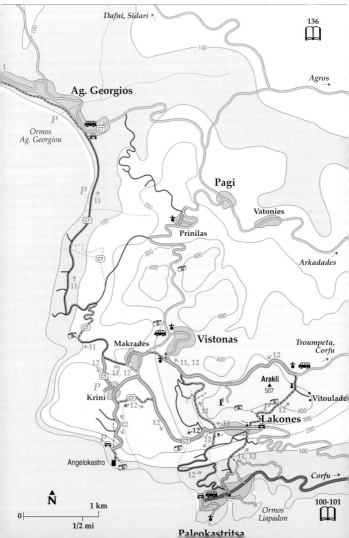

on page 86. When you reach the main road in **Lakones** (**40min**), turn right. Walk along the narrow street for 200m/yds, watching out for one-way traffic which is controlled by lights at each end of the village, then climb steps up to the left (just past a butcher's shop). In half a minute, where the alley bears right, keep climbing the steps, ignoring all side-alleys. In two minutes, at a T-junction at the top of the village, turn right uphill. This path, which is partly cobbled and with shallow steps, ascends up the SLOPES OF **Mt Arakli** (Picnic 12a). Follow the cobbled path away from the village, out onto the open hillside, with views down to the coast. After some zigzags the path levels out and soon turns inland. In 20 minutes you reach a stony track with a white OBELISK on your left (**1h10min**). This is the highest point on the walk, with Mt Arakli on the left. Turn left along the track and follow it downhill to the DOUKADES/VISTONAS ROAD (**1h15min**). There is a BUS SHELTER on the right, and an isolated church on a small hillside opposite is a prominent landmark.

Turn left and follow the road for 25 minutes, to the outskirts of Vistonas. As you near the village, you can take a short-cut by following a concrete lane to the left: it starts just past the **Vistonas** sign, beside a SHRINE at the side of the road and passes a CHURCH on the left. From the church keep straight downhill on a path through olive trees, rejoining the road after 200m/yds. Approaching the MAKRADES JUNCTION (**2h10min**), make a dash to the right, before the stall-keepers rush out to insist you taste their local wines from the barrel!

Continue through **Makrades** until, just past the last houses and a cafeneion, you come to a lane cutting across in front of you (concrete to the right and tarmac to the left). Head right along the concrete lane; the concrete soon turns to gravel. A few minutes down, a concrete lane joins the track from the left. Turn left on this lane (Walk 11 continues to the right here, down the track). Follow the lane through olive trees, then garden plots and vineyards, before climbing up to **Krini** (**2h20min**).

Entering the village you reach a T-junction with a narrow alley. You will turn left here, but why not first make a short diversion to the setting for Picnic 12b. Turn right and follow the alley for two minutes, to reach a beautiful stone-laid threshing floor just beyond the village. In spring this site is a mass of wild flowers, and there are seats from which you can contemplate the views

Krini from the threshing floor (Picnic 12b)

north along the western coastline. When you are ready to continue, return along the alley into the village centre, hardly a square, with a small tree in the middle. Turn right here, following the road to the outskirts of the village and continue straight on down the hill to Angelokastro.

Ten minutes downhill you're at the foot of a stumpy tower of scrub-covered rock, crowned by the castle ruins (reopened in 2009 after extensive renovation lasting eight years). Take the path leading off the parking area, and follow it to the top, keeping right at the fork three minutes up. From **Angelokastro** (Picnic 12c) the views are superb. You look along the escarpment wall as it slides off into a bay indented with sandy coves. On a clear day you can see across the island to Corfu Town — hence the strategic importance of this medieval fortress.

On the return to Krini, you can use paths to cut out some bends in the road (the paths are shown on the map). When you reach the top of the hill, on the village outskirts (before the first house on the right), turn right, down into an olive grove. There is a Corfu Trail marker on a telegraph pole at the start of this path. Follow this delightful path, gently descending, and when you meet a track in four minutes, turn left. One minute later, when the track ends, keep straight ahead along the path. In another four minutes descend into a dry stream bed. Turn left along the stream bed and, after a few metres, follow the path up to the right, out of the gully and onto the LAKONES ROAD (**3h**).

Turn right along the road. Some 15 minutes along (about five minutes past Taverna Bellavista — 'the best view in Europe'), descend steps alongside a shop on the right (ALKI'S ARTIST OLIVE WOOD PRODUCTION; **3h15min**). Two minutes down, ignore a faint fork off to the left. Follow this sometimes-overgrown path down to a concreted track. Continue down the track for some 40 minutes, all the way back to **Paleokastritsa**. The BUS STOP is a couple of minutes along to the right (**4h**) — or return to the CAR PARK at the foot of the monastery hill.

Walk 13: PALEOKASTRITSA • LIAPADES • GIANADES • ROPA PLAIN • SGOMBOU

See map pages 100-101; see photograph pages 32-33

Distance/time: 18.5km/11.5mi; 5h

Grade: moderate, with gradual ascents of about 350m/1150ft overall. There is a short, very awkward descent down a cleft near the start of the walk (dangerous if wet); less agile walkers should avoid this by starting out from the Elli Beach Hotel or Liapades.

Equipment: walking boots or stout shoes with good grip, sunhat, sunglasses, suncream, long-sleeved shirt, long trousers, raingear, swimwear, picnic, water

How to get there: 🚌 (journey 35min) or 🚐 to Paleokastritsa Camping
To return: 🚌 from Sgombou (Paleokastritsa bus), to Corfu Town (journey time 20min), or back to Paleokastritsa Camping for your car

Short walks

1 **Paleokastritsa — Liapades — Gianades:** 8.5km/5.3mi; 2h20min; Easy; equipment, access *by bus* as main walk; return by 🚌 from Gianades (not Sundays/holidays). Follow the main walk to Gianades.

2 **Paleokastritsa — Rovina Beach — Paleokastritsa:** 5km/3mi; 1h40min. Easy; equipment, access as main walk; return on the same bus or by car. Follow the main walk for a little over 30min — as far as the fork just after you leave the road at Villa Birlis. At the fork, bear right. Yellow arrows indicate the route. After heading behind a couple of buildings, the path swings abruptly left. Just after this, turn off to the right, and remain on this path, descending through a bosket of kermes oak, to the beach, ignoring paths off to the right. Return the same way.

Alternative walks

1 **Cape Ag Iliodoros:** 12km/7.5mi; 3h40min. Fairly strenuous, with a steep return ascent of 220m/720ft. Equipment/access as main walk. Follow the main walk to the 50min-point, then turn right on a track. After 40m, at a fork, go left. Keep to this track all the way to an isolated little cove on Cape Ag Iliodoros, 45 minutes downhill. Stupendous views across Liapades Bay await you. Return the same way, perhaps first visiting Limni Beach (shown on the cover); see the map.

2 **Marmaro Hills circuit:** 13km/8mi; 3h40min. Easy-moderate, with a gradual ascent of 250m/820ft. Equipment, access as main walk. Follow the main walk to the 55min-point, then go right (Corfu Trail). Walking through beautiful olive groves, circle the Marmaro Hills, terraced in tired stone walls. Stay on this main track, ignoring offshoots, until you meet a T-junction (1h35min). Turn left on this track. After 250m/yds the track describes a hairpin bend to the left; 150m/yds further on a track to the right leads to a TV mast, but you turn 90° left. Once more ignore offshoots. At the end of this track (a concrete block building is on the right), turn right and then immediately left. From this point occasional red arrows confirm that you are on the correct route. After some 15 minutes, ignore a track forking off right. Approaching the next junction (2h25min), keep right, soon enjoying a view of the escarpment wall cutting across the north of the island. Within the next 20 minutes, when a track (with a large water pipe alongside it) cuts across in front of you, turn hard left downhill to Liapades. On entering the village, continue to the right down a lane. When you meet a narrow road, follow it a short way left uphill, then take the first right and, at the end of this alley, descend to the right, to the village square (3h). Returning on the outward route, keep left at the bottom of the square.

M eander through mossy olive groves to the sound of chirping birds and, if you're unlucky, the blast of a shotgun — someone after those chirping birds. Cross a plain squared by ditches and cushioned in grass, with not an olive tree in sight. Plod along an open, shallow valley littered with scrub and trees. In spring, orchids, stars of Bethlehem, anemones and wild geraniums adorn this countryside. In autumn, the dry and faded, rocky hillsides are embellished with cyclamen and *Sternbergia,* the fields carpeted in squill and crocuses.

The walk starts at **Paleokastritsa** CAMPING. Head back along the main road towards Corfu Town. Some 80 paces beyond SUPERMARKET ARIS (just past a scooter rental shop), turn right on a concrete lane, part of the Corfu Trail. At the end of the lane pick up a path between two houses (signposted to the 'ACAPULCO' swimming pool). A couple of minutes across an olive grove, drop down onto a concrete lane, where the advertised pool is to your right. Cross the lane and climb some steps on the left. At the top, continue along the somewhat overgrown path to the right. Three minutes from the lane, you look straight down into a cleft in the ridge. Although only about 2m/6ft deep, it's steep — a very awkward descent. *Care and all fours are required. If at all wet it's dangerous! (You may find an old ladder here — or a rope; don't use either unless you're absolutely sure it will take your weight!)*

A steep descent on a path follows. Soon you overlook a cove set in rock walls. Ignore the path ascending to the left. The path emerges in the grounds of the ELLI BEACH HOTEL (**20min**). Walk to the left of the hotel and pool, to join a road. Head up the road and, shortly, turn left up steps, following Corfu Trail signposting through the terrace of the Cricketer's Taverna and then steps. Rejoining the road, after about 150m/yds climb steps up to the right (just past Villa Birlis, a small apartment block). Two minutes up, at a fork, go left. *(But for Short walk 2, go right here for Rovina Beach.)* On reaching a road, turn left. Almost immediately, at a fork, head right.

You now enter **Liapades** (**40min**), with its lovely manorial homes, handsome arched doorways and court-yards. Turn left at the T-junction, going downhill at first, and ignoring any turn-offs until you reach the square. With the church on the right, leave the square by heading uphill along the alley ahead (with a sign indicating 'no through road'). Again, ignore all turn-offs until, two minutes up, you come to a T-junction (just beyond a

Venetian manor on the left). Turn left here on a wide concrete path. A good five minutes up from the square, a country road cuts across in front of you; turn right. Two minutes along the road, where a track forks off to the right, keep left on the road (**50min**). *(But Alternative walk 1 heads right on the track.)*

Some five minutes later, at the next fork (by a SHRINE in a small upright concrete box; **55min**), keep left. *(But for Alternative walk 2, head right here.)* The way soon reverts from surfaced track to gravel. Within the next 15 minutes, leave the main track, which turns sharp left, and continue ahead on a lesser track, to ascend a gentle ridge. In 10 minutes the track fizzles out at a stone RUIN. Continue straight ahead off the track, following a faint path across an olive grove (*don't* take the wider path heading right). A minute downhill come onto a farm track and turn right. Several minutes (about 400m/yds) along the track, at a T-junction by a concrete block building on the left, turn left. Continue to ascend, now on the opposite side of the ridge.

The Ropa Valley comes into view through a V in the hills. Flat, herbaceous, and dotted with a few trees, it makes a complete transition in the landscape. Slightly further on, you look straight across the centre of the island. A descent follows, down a shallow side-valley. Some five minutes from the last junction, join a track before a bend and follow it to the right, heading down into the side-valley. *(Don't take the fainter track immediately to the right.)* In the distance stand the black mounds of Mt Ag Georgios near Vatos (Walk 15) and Ag Deka (Walk 16). Ten minutes along, ignore a faint track off to the left and, five minutes later, at a junction, keep right (but *ignore* the *faint* turn-off right just before this junction). Three minutes later a track joins you from the right. Looking across the valley you can see the church in Gianades. Knowing where you are heading, keep to the Corfu Trail (or use the map) through all the junctions. The Trail avoids the main roads in **Gianades** (**2h20min**) — but also misses the prettiest corner of the village, draped in bougainvillaea, near the church.

When you reach a T-junction with the Kanakades road on the far side of Gianades (**2h35min**), keep right. Just 100m/yds along, the ditch which has been on the right-hand side of the road passes under the road and emerges on the left. As soon as you cross this culvert, swing left on a farm track and head across the **Ropa Plain**.

Five minutes along, you cross a concrete culvert and a faint track joins you from the right. Keep ahead along the main track, which gradually softens into grass. Ahead and slightly off to your right are several large, isolated houses. Keep ahead on the grassy track until you meet another grassy track at a T-junction (nearly 20 minutes after leaving the road). There is a WIDE, DEEP DRAINAGE CHANNEL ahead of you. To continue you must cross this channel, which may carry water in spring.*

Out of the drainage channel, cross another track and then another bridge. Now keep straight ahead. When the track fades, make for the line of cypress trees not far ahead. Closer to the trees, you have to cross another couple of ditches. Then veer left, keeping in line with the cypress trees. When the line of cypresses ends, continue straight ahead in the same direction. Remaining in the grassy field, pick up a path which leads to a faint track, about three minutes from the cypresses. (In spring, when the grass is tall, this path is hardly visible.) Turn right on the track, up to the road (**3h25min**).

Turn right on the road and, after 30m/yds (just before a café), turn left on a narrow concrete lane with a GRASS-HOPPER SIGN at the turning. The concrete gives way to gravel and cuts through a ridge. You come into a very shallow valley, with an anarchy of vegetation. The escarpment wall reappears, filling the landscape to the north, with Skripero below.

Ten minutes from the turn-off, ignore a farm track off left (Walk 14). Three minutes later, where the track goes right to an isolated house, bear left on another track. After 100m/yds bear right along a fainter, earthen track, heading towards a row of pines. Pass through a gap in a hedge and join a stony track as you reach the pines. Now follow the track. A first pond appears over on your left. **Gavrolimni** (Picnic 13), the next pond, follows, almost hidden by the surrounding cultivation. The track briefly heads between high fences. Ignore two turn-offs to the right a few minutes later. On reaching a road, turn right. Entering the hamlet of **Trivouliattica** (**4h35min**), keep straight ahead. Continue north for 25 minutes, to the main Paleokastritsa road (BUS STOP), at **Sgombou** (**5h**).

*If you prefer not to paddle, follow this longer route (adds 30 minutes): turn right here, following the Corfu Trail south for five minutes, to a country road lined with eucalyptus trees. Turn left here for a little over 1km, to the Paleokastritsa road. Turn left again for another 1.2km, to reach the main route at the junction with the GRASSHOPPER SIGN.

Walk 14: SGOMBOU • DOUKADES • AG SIMEON • SGOMBOU

Distance/time: 25km/15.5mi; 8h

Grade: moderate but long, the only noticeable ascent being a steep climb of 150m/500ft to Doukades and Ag Simeon. You will need to be adventurous and have a good sense of direction beyond Doukades: some of the tracks and paths are hardly visible, especially in spring.

Equipment: walking boots or stout shoes with ankle support, sunhat, sunglasses, suncream, long-sleeved shirt, long trousers, raingear, picnic, plenty of water

How to get there and return: 🚌 (Paleokastritsa bus; journey time 20min) or 🚗 to/from Sgombou. Alight from the bus at the stop for the Lucciola Inn; motorists park by the side of the road near the inn.

Shorter walks

1 **Sgombou — Gavrolimni Pond — Doukades — Ag Simeon — Doukades — Paleokastritsa road:** 15km/9.5mi: 4h20min. Grade, equipment and access as above; return on the Paleokastritsa bus — to Corfu Town, or back to your car at Sgombou. Follow the main walk until you return to Doukades (4h05min). Leave the main walk here to return to the main road, 1km away (4h20min). Catch the bus across from the turn-off; it passes here 5min after departing Paleokastritsa.

2 **Doukades — Ag Simeon — Doukades — Sgombou:** 19.5km/12mi; 5h30min. Grade, equipment, access/return as main walk (take the Paleokastritsa bus to either Doukades turn-off; journey time 25min; travelling by car, park at the Lucciola Inn and pick up the bus there). From the bus stop, walk uphill to the village (1km/25min). Turn left at the first junction, then left again along an alley. Now pick up the main walk at the 3h-point (where the church door is on your right). Note comments under 'Grade' about the route beyond Doukades.

This is a hike full of bucolic charm. You pass by ponds, through thickets of tangled foliage, and cross grassy fields. On route you call at Ag Noufures, a charming abandoned monastery. An hour later, you climb an escarpment to the precariously-perched chapel of Ag Simeon, overlooking the turquoise waters of Liapades Bay. A striking panorama spreads out below you, and you can trace the route of the walk.

Start the walk in **Sgombou**. From the bus stop, cross the road, then turn right just past the mini-market, to reach the LUCCIOLA INN, an organic bistro (with rave reviews on Trip Advisor) that unfortunately had to close in autumn 2012. Motorists should park nearby. Continue up the road that passes to the left of the inn, towards the cypress trees. Follow this road to the hamlet of **Trivouliattica (25min)**. Here a road turns off left, but keep straight on past a set of children's swings, following more cypress trees. Follow this tarmac country road for 10 minutes, going under an overhead electricity line and passing scattered villas. On an uphill bend to the right (only 20m/yds past Villa Thea) turn left down a

Heron

stony track (there is a 3m/9ft-high concrete pillar with electricity meters on the left at the top of this track). Follow the gently meandering track downhill; after about 10 minutes you pass to the left of **Gavrolimni pond** where, for a short distance, the track is fenced off on both sides. In winter it's a good-sized pond, frequented by herons and, to a lesser extent, egrets and moorhens. Two large holly oaks at the side of the fenced track mark your approach to this pond. Crossing a broad plain, you'll see another pond over to your right (but in summer it will be dried up).

Continue along the track until it passes through a line of pretty pines. Some 30m/yds past the pines, bear right on a lesser, faint track which comes to a hedge gap after 100m/yds. Pass through the gap and follow the still-faint track across an open field, to a small house with a red pantiled roof. Join a track at the house and follow it to the left. Off to your left is a small farmstead with a jumble of derelict vehicles behind it. After the track breasts a small rise, there is a fenced-off grove of young olive trees on the hillside to your left.

Just after passing a stone and pantile barn on the right, turn right down a side-track signposted to CAMO-MILIA. Continue along this track until it nears Camomilia — a large, secluded country villa with an L-shaped swimming pool. Keep to the left outside the property's boundary fence, to join an indistinct and probably over-grown path. This leads you past another pond, below on your right. Follow this path as it gradually climbs the

In the grounds of Ag Noufures

shoulder of the hill and you reach **Ag Noufures (1h 30min)**. The gates of the churchyard are sometimes open. Inside the yard it's cool and fresh.

To continue the walk, stand with the belfry on your left, and head north along the crest, to reach a rough dirt track. Follow it to the right and head back down into the valley. Around 10 minutes from the *moni*, the track forks. Go right (more or less straight on). An old rusty barbed-wire fence runs along the right-hand side of the track. Minutes later you pass in front of a farm shed where

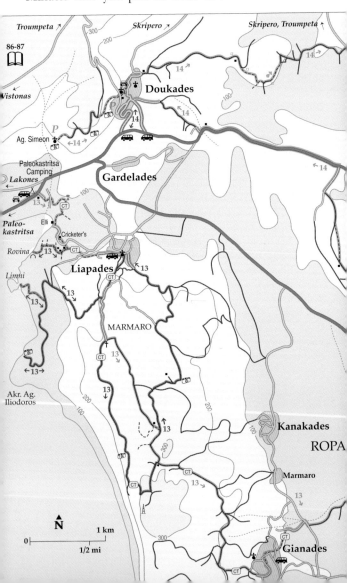

there may be loose dogs. Beyond the shed, continue on an old stone-laid trail that goes straight on. Ignore the farm track on the left. Minutes later, you join this farm track and head along it to the right. Three minutes later, a track joins from the right; keep left here. After a further three minutes, meet a private road and turn right along it. This road takes you in five minutes to the PALEOKASTRITSA ROAD (**2h**), where you turn left. The next half hour is spent on this busy road: take care, the locals treat it like the Monte Carlo strip!

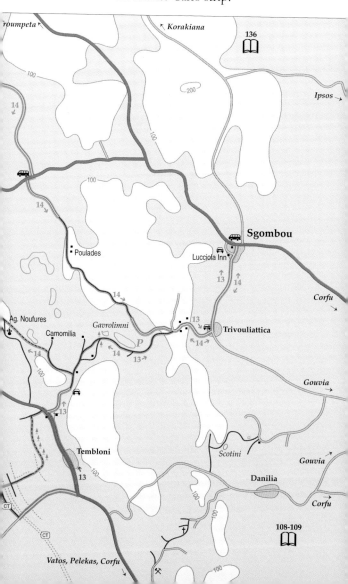

View over Liapades Bay from above the chapel of Ag Simeon

Walking towards the escarpment, you'll notice a rock face to the left. Above it sits a chapel — your eventual goal. But first make for Doukades. Turn off the main road on a sharp bend one minute past Villa Alexandra (a pretty cottage with a garden on the right, and a newer house alongside it). Where the road swings sharply down to the left, climb up right on a concrete lane. At the top of the rise, keep straight ahead along a stony track through cypress and olive groves. Ignore a fork off to the left a couple of minutes later. On meeting a tarred road, just where it reverts to gravel, turn left. This takes you in five minutes to the DOUKADES ROAD, where you turn right, immediately passing a road off to the left. Two minutes later, turn left up an alley into **Doukades**. This charming village is an artists' paradise.

A minute up, at a T-junction of paths, turn left and walk alongside a walled-in villa, with the front door of a CHURCH (**3h**) to your right. *(Shorter walk 2 and Picnic 14 join here.)* Cross a road and continue up the path (there may be a sign in German, 'Zur Kapelle', here). Turn off up the first narrow lane on the right. Leave the houses, following a cobbled path straight uphill (it may be covered in brushwood at first, and hard to locate). Within the first minute you cross a galvanised water pipe at an intersection, where you continue straight on, climbing steeply. When you meet a concrete lane, turn left uphill. The lane soon becomes a stony track. On the ascent you have stupendous views over Doukades, towards a valley clad in silvery-grey olive groves pierced with the dark spires of cypress trees (Picnic 14). There used to be wonderful views from the crest of the escarpment, but scrub has all but blocked them out.

Don't worry — a superb panorama awaits you later at Ag Simeon. About 10 minutes along the track you reach an unsigned fork. Take the left-hand fork; this descends gently at first, then soon rises. At the end of the track you're looking down on the chapel from the vantage point shown opposite. A minute down, at **Ag Simeon** (**3h40min**), a superb cliff-top panorama awaits you. Liapades is the larger village across from you; Gardelades is to the left. The Ropa Plain, a carpet of green in spring, slides into the central hills. In the distance, beyond the rolling wooded hills, sits Corfu Town. Paleokastritsa lies among the prominent headlands below.

From the chapel, return the same way to **Doukades**. On the descent you have a good view over this picturesque village. Back at the CHURCH (**4h05min**), keep straight ahead. *(But for Shorter walk 1, turn right, down to the Paleokastritsa road.)* You descend to the Skripero road, where you turn left. Two minutes through Doukades, opposite a house with an elaborate balcony, turn right down a concrete lane. Barely a minute down, you pass a large olive tree. Some 80m/yds beyond it, turn right on another lane which ascends the hillside. At the next fork, a couple of minutes further uphill, go left, entering an arboretum of summer shade.

Your next turn-off requires attention. It comes up about 10 minutes beyond this last fork. Watch out for an iron shed off the track to the left, followed by a farm building on the right; a minute later, just where the track swings sharp left, fork right (straight uphill) on a very old path

Flower-filled vineyards beyond Doukades

bounded by thick low STONE WALLS. You pass to the right of a SHED with a corrugated iron roof almost at once. Three minutes along, you're overlooking a small clearing on the edge of an olive grove. Here the path disappears into the grass. Facing the clearing, bear right (about 15°)

Green lizard

and head across the grove. A minute across, you regain the path lined with stone walls. It leads to a faint track, which you follow to the left. Half a minute along the track, at a four-way junction, turn left on another track (with cypress trees on your left and olive groves to the right). After 100m/yds, this track veers right, to head along the base of a ridge. Continue along the track, which soon peters out, and in two minutes, pass an open-sided barn with concrete posts on the right. Keep straight ahead (now on a barely-discernible track), soon passing an open WELL. Ascending slightly, the track becomes clearer. When it forks, keep left (ie, straight on). A minute later, at a T-junction, turn right downhill, after 50m/yds joining a track coming from the right. Heading along to the left, squeeze by a gate across the track. The countryside is lush with trees and bushes, swallowing up the fields and plots. A few minutes along, a track joins from the left, and a minute later you join a more substantial track coming from the right. Turn left along this track, past a vineyard and market garden, and ascend a small hill. Keep along the main track until you meet a small COUNTRY ROAD (**5h15min**). Turn right and follow this road for 45 minutes, to the PALEOKASTRITSA ROAD (**6h**).

If your legs are sending you messages, you can catch a bus here. To head on, cross the road, and walk along it to the right. After 130m/yds, turn left uphill on a minor road. When the tarmac ends after about 10 minutes, keep straight ahead on the main track. Continue uphill until you go over a crest; then, after passing a smallholding in the trees, you descend to a tarmac road (slightly downhill to your right). Turn left on this road and follow it downhill to arrive back at the turn-off to Gavrolimni pond (your outgoing route). Remain on the road back to **Trivouliattica** (**7h30min**) and then walk ahead to **Sgombou** (**8h**).

Walk 15: GOUVIA • ROPA PLAIN • VATOS • MIRTIOTISSA BEACH • GLYFADA

See also photograph pages 32-33
Distance/time: 13.8km/8.5mi; 3h50min

Grade: moderate, with an ascent of 200m/650ft above Vatos and a steep descent of 50m/150ft on the last stretch to the beach at Glyfada.

Equipment: walking boots or shoes with good grip, sunhat, sunglasses, suncream, long-sleeved shirt, long trousers, raingear, swimwear, picnic, water

How to get there: 🚌 to Gouvia (Dasia bus; journey time 20min). Alight just before the traffic lights on the main road, opposite Diella's Discount Centre.
To return: 🚌 from Glyfada; journey time 40min

Short walk: Vatos — Trialos — Mirtiotissa Beach — Glyfada: 5.5km/3.5mi; 2h. Grade and equipment as main walk. Access: 🚌 or 🚗 to Vatos (Glyfada bus); alight from the bus at the Vatos/Glyfada junction; park near the petrol station. Return as main walk — back to base, or back to your car at Vatos. Walk from the bus stop along to the tiny souvenir shop (closed at present) on the left, just before the petrol station. Here turn left, following the main walk from just after the 2h05min-point to the end. *To make this even shorter and avoid the climb:* Do *not* turn right past the school in three minutes, but carry on along the village road for another 250m to a fork, with a memorial and church on the left and a bus stop on the right. Go right here. After five minutes, at the end of the village, there is a church with white-walled cemetery on the left. On the right, opposite the cemetery there's a small patch of greenery, at the end of which a narrow but clear path leads into some shady olive groves. This undulating path takes you to the Mirtiotissa access road in 15 minutes. Follow the route down to the beach and pick up the walk at the 3h20min-point. *This route can also be used to make a circuit*: To access the path from the beach, note that it leaves the road *past* the bend to the right, on a left-hand bend.

Alternative walk: Gouvia — Scotini Pond — Ropa Plain — Vatos: 8.25km/5mi; 2h10min. Easy; stout shoes will suffice; access by 🚌 as main walk; return bus from Vatos (Glyfada bus). Follow the main walk to Vatos and keep on the main road past the petrol station. Catch the bus at the Pelekas/Glyfada junction, on the Corfu Town side of the road.

Cross the island from east to west and discover the diversity of Corfu's landscapes. Within a stone's throw of Gouvia's tourist haunts, you're in the countryside. Half an hour brings you to quiet rolling hills. You come upon a large pond full of terrapin and frogs, in an enchanting valley. Heading west, you cross the Ropa Plain — with a mere scattering of trees, it sits like an airfield, buried below hills. Ascending the slopes of Ag Georgios, the west coast unravels — in complete contrast to the east.

Scotini Pond

105

Terrapin

Vivid green pines fleck the rocky sea-cliffs towering above some of the island's most beautiful beaches — the most spectacular being Mirtiotissa.

  Start the walk at the bus stop in **Gouvia**; it is located on the main road (dual carriageway) just before the traffic lights. Carefully cross this road; then skirt the left side of DIELLA'S DISCOUNT CENTRE, to join a country road (do *not* bear left on the other road to Danilia, the folklore village). At the third turning on the left, there is a sign, 'VILLA JASMIN' (**10min**): turn left here. Keep to this lane for just under 1km; then, on crossing a low crest, take the *second* track turning down to the left, passing a house on your right. Skirting a fenced-off field, descend into a gentle open valley. Five minutes off the road, you're overlooking **Scotini**, the pond shown on page 105 — unless it's high summer!

  A minute past the pond, head left at a junction. Ignore a fork to the left almost immediately and soon reach a ROAD (**40min**). Turn left and, four minutes along, take a side-road off to the right, soon passing a few country villas in nice gardens. A little over 10 minutes along, at a junction, fork right (slightly uphill).

Continue along this road all the way to the end of the tarmac, where you turn sharp left onto a gravel track (there is a sign, 'VATOS-ROPA', on the gateway of a small market garden on the right). You soon pass a house on the right, behind a wall, with a shrine in the garden.

Soon you're descending into the **Ropa Valley**. Just after ignoring a faint farm track off to the right, come to a junction, where a wide track cuts across in front of you: follow it to the right. The Ropa Valley begins appearing in bits and pieces, over the trees. Gianades is the village visible midway up the Marmaro Hills, across the plain. Five minutes from the junction you join a track coming from the right. Keep left here (the surface becomes tarred almost immediately) and pass a few houses. A working quarry has eaten away half of the hillside on the left. Five minutes along the road, you emerge on the quarry road and turn right. Minutes down you're on the CORFU/LIAPADES ROAD (**1h35min**), where you turn right.

From here you cross the **Ropa Plain**. Some 40m/yds along the road, turn left on a farm track that strikes across the plain. In spring the grass is knee-high and full of flowers. *Attention:* this track ends at what *may* be a military installation; I may be wrong, but *don't take any*

photographs around here or your film may be confiscated.

Continue to the right of the enclosure, on a fainter track which soon runs into a field. Looking ahead, you can see the village of Vatos, your next objective, strung out along the lower slopes of Ag Georgios. Some 20 minutes along, you reach another wide DRAINAGE DITCH. At this point you join the Corfu Trail (southbound) and you will be with it as far as Mirtiotissa. It's likely that you'll spot some birds

Mirtiotissa Beach (Picnic 15)

now: crested larks, red storks, goldfinches, stonechats, whinchats. Turn left and keep along the bank, with the wide ditch on your right. You soon join a gravel track (the ditch now almost resembling a canal), and you will pass several steel bridges linking the golf course on each side the the canal. Keep along the track, cross a concrete slab bridge, and soon pass the GOLF COURSE CLUBHOUSE on the opposite bank. When you meet the ERMONES ROAD, close to the entrance to the golf club, on the outskirts of **Vatos** (**2h05min**), turn left.

Two minutes along (less than 100m past a Shell PETROL STATION), turn right on a narrow tarred road. *(The Short walk begins here; the Alternative walk keeps ahead to the Pelekas/Glyfada junction.)* A couple of minutes uphill, the road veers sharply left, in front of a house. Some 30m/yds beyond the house, go right on a path bordered by high fences. Following this old village path, you come out on a village road, five minutes from the main road. Head right and, in two minutes, turn left uphill into the TOP PART OF **Vatos** (**2h20min**). After 160m/yds you pass a small square on the right. After another 160m/yds, take the next road on the right (with an information board at its start). It doubles back momentarily, passes the village school, and heads uphill.

The track climbs steadily on the lower flanks of **Mt Ag Georgios**. Shortly after passing two RADIO MASTS, you round the nose of the ridge and look down onto a beryl sea, as the hillside plummets to the rocks below. Further along the track, look back for the spectacular views along the hilly coastline. Fifteen minutes into the descent, the track forks. Descend to the left, passing the scant remains of the abandoned hamlet of **Tria-**

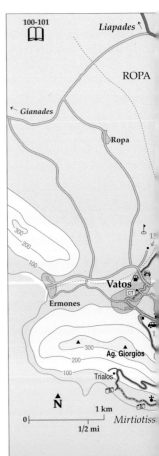

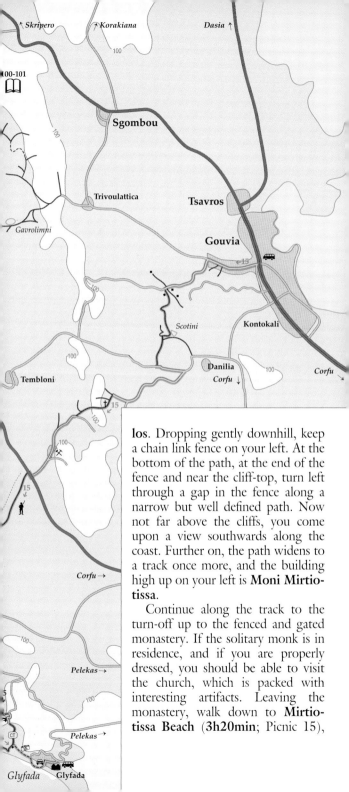

los. Dropping gently downhill, keep a chain link fence on your left. At the bottom of the path, at the end of the fence and near the cliff-top, turn left through a gap in the fence along a narrow but well defined path. Now not far above the cliffs, you come upon a view southwards along the coast. Further on, the path widens to a track once more, and the building high up on your left is **Moni Mirtiotissa**.

Continue along the track to the turn-off up to the fenced and gated monastery. If the solitary monk is in residence, and if you are properly dressed, you should be able to visit the church, which is packed with interesting artifacts. Leaving the monastery, walk down to **Mirtiotissa Beach** (**3h20min**; Picnic 15), backed by towering pine-clad cliffs. From late autumn until spring attractive streamlets cascade down these rocky walls, and the beach is as idyllic as it looks in the photo on pages 106-107. But in summer it's packed out, and you may not see the sand for beach umbrellas.

Heading on to Glyfada, follow the steep track from Mirtiotissa Beach. Close on 10 minutes uphill, just after an S-bend and once through the car park of the roadside taverna, descend a track on your right. This runs through a grove of olive trees, towards a restaurant/bar set back in the trees (closed at time of writing). Keep to the left of a small toilet block and take the path ahead, running between two fences. *(Do not* descend to the right.) Crossing a small flat area, you overlook Glyfada's wide beach — another stupendous setting below cliffs studded with beautiful, fluffy pines. But alas, a large hotel and apartment blocks have blighted its natural beauty.

Dropping down off this flat-topped clearing, you follow a watercourse and drop very steeply downhill. Take care, as the descent is stony. Three minutes down you emerge at the back of a restaurant. From here, descend steps at the side of the restaurant to the BEACH at **Glyfada** (**3h40min**). Head along the beach to the left for five minutes, then ascend a wide road to a large car park. Continue up the road for five minutes, to the junction above the hotel, where the bus turns around (**3h50min**).

Walk 16: ANO GAROUNA • MONI AG DEKA • WATERWORKS GARDEN • BENITSES

Photos page 36 and opposite   **Distance/time:** 7km/4.5mi; 2h25min

Grade: moderate, with an ascent of 280m/920ft on a clear but fairly overgrown path and a rather steep descent of 580m/1900ft

Equipment: walking boots, sunhat, sunglasses, suncream, long-sleeved shirt, long trousers (for protection from thorny scrub as well as the sun), fleece, raingear, swimwear, picnic, water

How to get there: 🚌 to Ano Garouna; journey time 40min
To return: 🚌 from Benitses; journey time 30min

Short walk: Ano Garouna — Moni Ag Deka — Ano Garouna: 3.5km/2mi; 1h25min. Moderate ascent/descent of 280m/920ft (as above). Equipment and access as main walk; return on the same bus (or 🚗: park in the car park below Ano Garouna). Follow the main walk to the 45min-point and return the same way.

Alternative walk: See Alternative walk 17-2 on page 114.

Mt Ag Deka, Corfu's second-highest peak (576m/ 1890ft), is a pint-sized mountain rising in the centre of the island. Atop it lies a shallow depression, the crater of an ancient volcano according to folklore. In the depression you find a rival for the Garden of Eden — an unkempt orchard boasting some 45 different varieties of fruits. Tucked away on the summit, behind creepered walls, sits the monastery *(moni)* of Pantokrator of Ag Deka, a cool, shady sanctuary. Both ascending and descending, you enjoy a magnificent panorama of the inland hills and vales edging out to the coasts, before they climb and tumble into the sea. Nearer the shore, you stumble onto an overgrown garden. This, surprisingly, is the waterworks, built over 150 years ago to furnish Corfu Town with water. On this walk we will be sharing part of the route with the Corfu Trail.

Start the walk at the BUS SHELTER/CAR PARKING AREA below **Ano Garouna**. Facing the village above, take a path ascending to the right, to the village centre. The path emerges just below a restaurant (currently closed). Continue up between the houses. Then take the first left (the alley to the right at this point leads past a couple of very old *cafeneions* and on to the village square). Keep left again almost immediately. At the next fork, keep right. This turn takes you out of the village. On coming to another fork (beside a large olive tree), go left. Three minutes out of the village, you pass above a stone farm shed and, five minutes further up, a road comes into sight not far above. Scramble up the hillside

Left: gathering chestnuts in autumn at Moni Pantokrator of Ag Deka (Walk 16)

to this concrete road and follow it to the left for 20m/yds. Then climb up the steep embankment on your right, where the path is not obvious. In a couple of minutes you reach a stone-laid track, where you turn right uphill. When this track ends, continue on the overgrown path that leads off it. The path is always distinct, but you will have to push your way through encroaching vegetation.   Climbing, the views expand as far north as Pantokrator. A steady ascent brings you to a JUNCTION (**40min**) The village of Ag Deka (visited later in the walk) is down to the left; Moni Ag Deka is up to the right. Head right, passing an orchard of cherry and walnut trees, and enter the courtyard of **Moni Ag Deka** (**45min**). You are now in the shallow 'crater', but almost unaware of it. The chapel is usually locked; the monks' quarters are now used only for storage, or when a local festivity takes grip of the site. You can quench your thirst at the well — unless it, too, is locked.

Return to the junction below the *moni* and keep straight on (right) for the village of Ag Deka. Ten minutes downhill on this partly-cobbled path you pass a prominent rock — an excellent viewpoint. You look straight down onto the lagoon near the airport. Villages encircled by olive groves lie scattered amidst the hills. The prominent white building down to the right is the Achilleion Palace. Soon you will reach a raw bulldozed stone and earth track. Turn left downhill, round an S-bend, and keep descending. Two minutes down the track, turn sharp right on a narrower track. Then, after just 50m/yds, watch for a boulder with a red arrow: this alerts you to your ongoing path which drops steeply down to the left, with olive trees up to your right and a chain link fence on the left. Keep descending, following the fence round to the left (where another path joins from the right). Some 20m/yds downhill, turn right (with another fence on your left). Cross a water pipe and continue downhill, shortly descending some rough steps leading down to a parking area. Turn right immediately above the car park, along a concrete path leading in less than 100m/yds into the VILLAGE OF **Ag Deka**. Keep ahead along the narrow alleys, and in three minutes you will emerge on the road (**1h25min**).

Turn right on the road. A good five minutes along, as you leave the village and just after rounding a bend, you pass a large shrine built into a retaining wall on the right. Some 40m/yds past the shrine turn left downhill on a

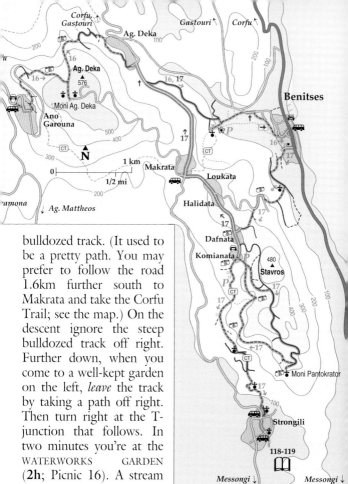

bulldozed track. (It used to be a pretty path. You may prefer to follow the road 1.6km further south to Makrata and take the Corfu Trail; see the map.) On the descent ignore the steep bulldozed track off right. Further down, when you come to a well-kept garden on the left, *leave* the track by taking a path off right. Then turn right at the T-junction that follows. In two minutes you're at the WATERWORKS GARDEN (**2h**; Picnic 16). A stream runs down the valley floor, which is a lush, exuberant tangle of vegetation.

Return to the T-junction and now keep straight on, through orchards and vegetable gardens. A causeway takes you to a road. Walk right along the road for a minute, then descend steps alongside a garish shrine. Follow the path below the shrine, bearing left into the trees. The path emerges on the road to the water treatment works. Turn right down the concrete road for 40m/yds, then turn left down a path opposite the gated entrance to the works. Passing the cemetery, you join a narrow road at a tree-shaded parking area next to a stream. Cross the stream and continue along a narrow street through the old village. This leads you to the main square at **Benitses**, opposite the harbour (**2h25min**). You can take any bus (green or blue) on the sea side of the main road.

Walk 17: BENITSES • DAFNATA • STRONGILI

See map page 113 **Distance/time:** 10km/6.25mi; 3h20min

Grade: strenuous, with an ascent of 400m/1300ft and descent of 400m/1300ft (dangerous if wet)

Equipment: walking boots or stout shoes with grip and ankle support, sunhat, sunglasses, suncream, long-sleeved shirt, long trousers, fleece, raingear, swimwear, picnic, water

How to get there: 🚌 to Benitses; journey time 30min
To return: 🚌 from Strongili; journey time 1h

Short walk: Komianata — Moni Pantokrator — Komianata: 3.8km/2.4mi; 1h20min. Moderate; overall ascent of 100m/330ft; some paths are very rocky. Access by 🚌 or 🚗 to Komianata (park just before the road ends, but do not obstruct the bus turning bay). Follow the main walk from the 1h15min-point to the 2h35min-point.

Alternative walks

1 Benitses — Dafnata — Moni Pantokrator — Benitses: 9.5km/6mi; 3h35min. Grade, equipment and access as main walk; return on the same bus (or 🚗 to/from Benitses; park in the large seafront car park). Follow the main walk to Moni Pantokrator, then return to Dafnata and take your outgoing path back to Benitses.

2 Benitses — Dafnata — Moni Pantokrator — Ag Deka — Benitses: 14.6km/9.1mi; 4h20min. Grade, equipment and access as main walk; return on the same bus (or 🚗 to/from Benitses; park in the large seafront car park). The circuit takes in the uphill part of the main walk, then follows quiet country roads linking several hillside villages, and ends by following the downhill part of Walk 16 to Benitses. Follow the main walk to the 2h35min-point. Then walk back along the road, through Dafnata and Halidata. When you reach the Ag Deka/Strongili road after just under 2km, turn right and follow it to the southern outskirts of Ag Deka village. Look out for a little garden called the 'Love Nest' on the left side of the road, just before a shrine set into the roadside wall. The path down to Benitses is opposite this garden, on the right. Pick up Walk 16 at the 1h25min-point and follow it via the waterworks garden, back to Benitses.

Winding up through cypresses and olive groves, you climb to the hillside village of Dafnata, trailing superb coastal scenery behind you. The village sits high and fast on table-topped Mt Stavros. Across the mountain stands the little chapel of Pantokrator. Between Komianata and Strongili our walk coincides with the Corfu Trail for most of the way.

Start the walk at **Benitses**: head south along the main road. Just after passing the Hotel Potamaki on the right, turn right on a road. (A yellow dot marks this turn-off.) On coming to a T-junction running parallel with a ditch (**2min**), turn left. Then, 30m/yds along, go left on a path. Yellow dots reappear. Barely a minute along the path, just after a fenced-off olive grove, ascend steps to the right. At the top of the the steps the path swings left. At another junction (by an electricity pole), turn right up a cobbled path, as indicated by a yellow

Moni Pantokrator

arrow. Ignore a turn-off to the right; remain on the cobbled path, to round the hillside above Benitses. Three minutes past the turn-off, a fence is on your left. The way fades as you climb: be sure to keep to the right of the olive grove.

On meeting a CON-CRETED TRACK (**30min**), turn left. Five minutes along, turn right on the drive up to a chapel, where a refreshing, cool spring in the shade of an enormous oak tree awaits you. Moving on, follow the path below the chapel courtyard, heading round the hillside and crossing a dry stream bed. Five minutes after leaving the chapel, the path climbs to a tarmac road. Turn right on this road and, where it bends left, there is a lovely view down over Benitses and along the coast to Corfu Town.

Continue uphill through pine woods and, where the road enters an olive grove, keep a sharp lookout for a path on the left. Follow this path steeply uphill, climbing through cypress trees. Five minutes up the path, watch for a fork and head right, steeply uphill, on a zigzag path. When you meet a track, bear right along it; this track soon becomes a concrete lane leading you steeply up to the road at **Dafnata** — where there is a lovely viewpoint overlooking Corfu Town and the east coast. An old millstone acts as a table, and there are several seats. Turn left along the road through the village, to reach the small hamlet of **Komianata**. Continue straight ahead along an alley, to reach the tiny square, with a small tree in the middle (**1h15min**).

As soon as you enter the square, take the first path left uphill (at the *top* of the square). Then turn right immediately, making your way behind the houses, to begin the ascent of Mt Stavros. Soon there is a superb outlook across the centre of the island (one setting for Picnic 17). Two minutes along the path, ignore a turn-off to the

115

right (your return route). At this point, do a short zigzag uphill by turning left, then, after a few metres/yards, bearing off right, continuing uphill. Your destination is the hilltop slightly to the right. Ignore another, faint fork to the left barely two minutes further on. Keep beside a fenced-off area, rounding the hillside. When you reach a track, turn right along it and follow it across the shoulder of **Mt Stavros**, ignoring tracks off left and right.

Soon after passing between some hillside vegetable plots, the track begins to descend and you will shortly spot **Moni Pantokrator (2h)** below you on the right. The building stands on a rocky outcrop at the end of the track, hanging out over the Messongi Valley. Inside the chapel are some barely-discernible frescoes and a fine canvas. Before heading on, get your bearings. Facing the track, look left, to see your return route below, running along the slopes of Mt Stavros. Then head back up the track for 25m/yds and take a path descending to the left (beside a large rock). Ignore a fork off left two minutes down. Circling the mountainside, you catch sight of Strongili below. Half an hour from the chapel, ignore a faint turn-off to the left. (It's a short-cut to the Strongili path below, but is overgrown.) Coming into olive groves again, keep uphill to the right, soon rejoining your outgoing path, where you turn left. Two minutes down, you're back at the square in **Komianata (2h35min)**.

Descending to Strongili, head left from the bottom of the square, following a yellow arrow. A stony path takes you down into cypresses (another setting for Picnic 17). Keep to the main path, passing some iron sheds on your right and ignoring any paths to the right. Ten minutes from the square (well under 1km), above a roofless stone building down to the right, keep left at a fork. At the next fork, five minutes later, go right. Shortly, Strongili reappears. Five minutes from the last fork, you pass a CHAPEL on your right, meet a track and follow it to the left. The track forks immediately: keep right downhill. In five minutes, when the track forks again, go right and, metres downhill, go left on a sometimes cobbled path (yellow arrow on a tree). Passing an abandoned CHAPEL on your left, the path runs to the right of a GATE and FENCED-OFF ORANGE GROVE. *(The Corfu Trail markers are often removed here!)* Meeting a track beside another CHURCH, follow it to the STRONGILI ROAD. Flag down a bus here or, better, turn left into **Strongili (3h20min)**, where there is a choice of cafés as well as a bus stop.

Walk 18: MESSONGI • AG DIMITRIOS • HLOMOS • KOUSPADES • KORAKADES • PETRETI • PERIVOLI

See also photograph page 40

Distance/time: 14.5km/9mi; 4h

Grade: easy to moderate; steep ascent of 300m/1000ft at the start

Equipment: stout shoes, sunhat, sunglasses, suncream, long-sleeved shirt, long trousers, raingear, swimwear, picnic, water

How to get there: 🚌 to Messongi (or Kavos bus to Messongi); journey time 45min; or 🚗 to Messongi; park along the seafront, inside the village, at the side of the main south road.

To return: 🚌 from Perivoli; journey time 1h05min, back to Corfu Town, or to your car at Messongi

Alternative walk: Hlomos — Kouspades — Korakades — Petreti — Notos — Boukari — Hlomos: 11.5km/7.1mi; 2h45min. Easy-moderate, with overall descent/ascent of 220m/720ft. Equipment as main walk. Access: 🚌 or 🚗 to Hlomos (park in the car park or at the entrance to the village). Start at the church: follow the main walk from the 1h20min-point to the cove of Notos. Then return around the headland to Petreti. Cross the beach, pass the fishing harbour, and take the road along the coast. Follow this for 2km, to arrive at sandy Boukari Beach. Now follow the road up to Kouspades and, at the top of the hill, turn right, to retrace your outgoing route back to Hlomos.

This walk may not appeal to everyone because of the road-walking. But outside peak season these roads carry only a trickle of traffic, and several users have told us how much they enjoyed the walk. Charming villages and hamlets lie on route; each has its own personality. They adorn ridges, step hillsides, and dribble down slopes to the sea. You wind your way around the sylvan, seaward slopes, through olive groves and down lanes of cypress trees. Seascapes ebb and flow.

Start out at the bus stop/turnaround in **Messongi**. Walk back the way the bus came into the village and, at the T-junction (**2min**), turn left towards Ag Dimitrios. Follow the road uphill past Kato Spilion, a small village on a side-road off to the right. On arriving at the village of **Ag Dimitrios** (**55min**), the road swings left to Hlomos. But before heading along it, continue up to the right for a minute — to enjoy a superb panorama encompassing the central mountains, the gulf and the Pantokrator hills. Returning to the Hlomos road, follow it for a little over 1km, then take first turn-off left — up to the top of this cascading village. Two minutes up, turn

Hlomos

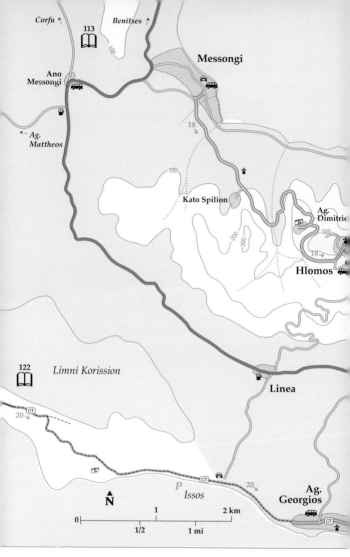

right along a lane; it curves left, passing below the church. From the CHURCH at **Hlomos** (**1h20min**; Picnic 18a) there are fine views along the northern coastline to Mt Pantokrator, and south to the tip of the island.

Leaving the church, head back along the lane, then take the first alley off left, following a sign for TAVERNA SIRTAKI. Old houses flank the alley. A minute down, either head right to the taverna or turn left and then go right immediately, to descend to the village square, a minute below. On reaching the narrow square, continue straight downhill. (Coming from the taverna, this is the first right turn out of the square.) Half a minute down from the square, descend steps to the right, then continue along the path, down into a gully. The way heads along the side of a steep embankment. *Keep an eye on red and blue dots marking the route.* Eight minutes down, at a fork just past a shed on the right, keep left. Two minutes later, keep right at the next fork. A minute later, by

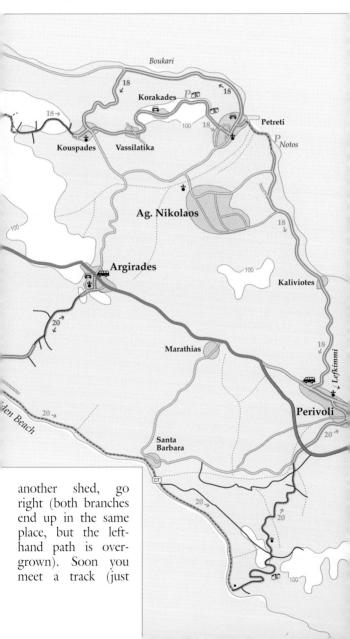

another shed, go right (both branches end up in the same place, but the left-hand path is overgrown). Soon you meet a track (just where it veers off to the left). Continue straight ahead along this track. Just after a fork off to the right, at a junction, again continue straight on, ignoring the fork to the left. You pass through **Kouspades** (**2h**), a picture-postcard village. Just outside it, at a junction, go right, then left after 50m/yds. Some five minutes later, pass through **Vassilatika**.

Continue along the road into **Korakades**, where you turn right along the village lane. An air of abandon hangs over this farming settlement. Soon the lane veers sharp left. Descending past derelict houses (Picnic 18b), you wind your way down the hillside, with tremendous views through the trees on the left over to the hills of Epirus.

A good 10 minutes down, meet a road on the outskirts of the small fishing village of **Petreti**. Cross the road and continue downhill on a road more or less opposite. A minute later, you cross the road again. At the bottom of the road, bear left. Then, 100m/yds along, take the road forking off right, down to a mud-flat beach (**2h55min**). Now turn right along the seafront and continue along the beach, crossing two streams (no footbridges). At the far end of the beach, follow a path through an olive grove over a low headland and on to the pretty cove of **Notos** (Picnic 18c).

Climb a short concrete lane, to join a tarmac road at the crest. Continue along the coast road and, 10 minutes later, at a T-junction, turn left, still following he coast. Just over 1km from the T-junction, the road turns inland, to **Perivoli** (**4h**). The BUS STOP is in front of the cafés and bars, just to the right of the T-junction.

Old bridge over the canal at the Korission Lagoon (the 1h45min-point in Walk 20), with Mt Ag Mattheos (Walk 19) in the background

Walk 19: MT AG MATTHEOS

Photograph page 24 (photographs of Mt Ag Mattheos page 15 and opposite)

Distance/time: 6km/3.75mi; 2h05min

Grade: strenuous, with an ascent of 300m/1000ft on a motorable track and a descent of 300m/1000ft on a rocky path and track

Equipment: walking boots, sunhat, sunglasses, suncream, long-sleeved shirt, long trousers, raingear, picnic, plenty of water

How to get there and return: 🚌 to/from Ag Mattheos village; journey time 50min, or 🚗: park on the main road south of the village, near the gnome garden where the walk begins.

The panoramic view over the south of the island from Mt Ag Mattheos is well worth the climb. It's best done in the late afternoon, when it's cooler and the light is softer. While the track that you follow on the ascent is wide and ugly, scarring the whole mountainside, the descent path through the kermes oak wood (one of the few left on the island), is ample compensation.

Start the walk in the village of **Ag Mattheos**, outside the cafés and restaurants on the main road. Follow the main road south for a little over five minutes. Near the end of the village, just past a house on the right, turn right up a lane (walkers' signpost). As soon as you turn off you'll spot a garden with gnomes — Snow White and the Seven Dwarfs! Ignore the turn-off to the right soon afterwards. Soon concrete comes underfoot, then gravel. Two more tracks join from the right within the first 10 minutes: continue straight uphill. At the next fork, at a metal barrier, go straight on (to the left is the original mountain track, now partly bulldozed away).

Ascending, there is a good outlook over the thickly-wooded Messongi basin below. Higher up, you enjoy a bird's-eye view over the village of Ag Mattheos, then Messongi Bay. The east coast slowly unravels and, on a bend, you look out over the Korission Lagoon (**50min**). Soon the kermes oak wood closes in around you. The last section of track is concreted.

Just below the summit you reach **Moni Pantokrator** (**1h10min**). Standing on the track below the walled compound, pick up the path that climbs to the left of the *moni* and to three rather dilapidated lookout points, the first with a hut on stilts overlooking the west coast. Continue beyond the trig point in a ruined walled enclosure at the SUMMIT OF **Mt Ag Mattheos** to a seat overlooking the east coast and another seat further on, with southerly views to both coasts and Lake Korission. In October the rocky hilltop is a mass of cyclamen

121

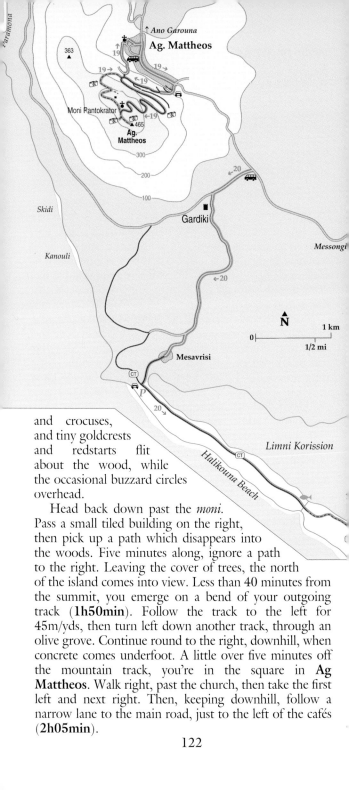

and crocuses, and tiny goldcrests and redstarts flit about the wood, while the occasional buzzard circles overhead.

Head back down past the *moni*. Pass a small tiled building on the right, then pick up a path which disappears into the woods. Five minutes along, ignore a path to the right. Leaving the cover of trees, the north of the island comes into view. Less than 40 minutes from the summit, you emerge on a bend of your outgoing track (**1h50min**). Follow the track to the left for 45m/yds, then turn left down another track, through an olive grove. Continue round to the right, downhill, when concrete comes underfoot. A little over five minutes off the mountain track, you're in the square in **Ag Mattheos**. Walk right, past the church, then take the first left and next right. Then, keeping downhill, follow a narrow lane to the main road, just to the left of the cafés (**2h05min**).

Walk 20: GARDIKI CASTLE • KORISSION LAGOON • AG GEORGIOS • GOLDEN BEACH • PERIVOLI

Map begins opposite, ends on pages 118-119; see photographs pages 15, 40, 120

Distance/time: 22.5km/14mi; 6h10min

Grade: easy; mostly along a beach … but plodding over sand is tiring. Steep climb of 100m/330ft to Perivoli. *Virtually no shade en route.*

Equipment: as little as possible! Light trainers for reaching and leaving beaches (and the odd stretch of rock), sunhat, sunglasses, high-protection suncream, swimwear, picnic, plenty of water

How to get there: 🚌 to the Gardiki turn-off (Ag Mattheos bus); journey time 45min. Or 🚌 or 🚗 to Messongi (park on the main road, just outside the centre of Messongi) and taxi to 'Lake' Korission. (Motorists who just want a stroll can park down by the lagoon.) *The ideal scenario would be for friends to drop you at the northern end of the lagoon and collect you later at Perivoli.*

To return: 🚌 from Perivoli — back to Corfu Town; journey time 1h05min, or back to your 🚗 at Messongi or Ano Messongi

Shorter walks

1 **Gardiki Castle — Ag Georgios — Argirades:** 15km/9.5mi; 4h. Easy; equipment and access as main walk; return by bus from Argirades (back to Corfu Town or back to your car). Follow the main walk to Golden Beach, then walk along the country road to Argirades (sign-posted five minutes past the church in Ag Georgios, just before Golden Beach; see map on pages 118-119). On entering Argirades, keep straight ahead to the church square. Then turn left and, when you reach the main road, follow it uphill for 100m/yds. The bus stops in front of the first large olive tree on the left.

2 **Argirades — Golden Beach — Perivoli:** 12km/7.5mi; 3h45min. Grade and equipment as main walk. Access: Kavos 🚌 or 🚗 to Argirades (park at the side of the main road, near the turn-off for Kous-pades and Petreti). Start out at the turn-off for Kouspades and Petreti. Take the lane diagonally opposite, heading into the church square in Argirades. Beyond the church go right. Ignore a fork off to the right, and remain on this small country road all the way to Golden Beach (see map on pages 118-119). Join the main walk at the 3h10min-point and follow it to the end. Return as the main walk — back to Corfu Town, or back to your car at Argirades.

Almost all of this walk (much of which we share with the Corfu Trail) extends along the seashore — a seemingly-endless sandy beach. 'Lake' Korission, where you first meet the sea, is a shallow lagoon bordered by a causeway of sand dunes. Traipsing across these dunes you pass through an enchanting thicket of holly oak, an pretty interlude before you come upon the *real* dunes — billows of golden sand splashed with silver-green clumps of juniper. Ag Georgios briefly disrupts the landscape as you cut off a corner of rocky coastline to rejoin the shore. The dunes now behind you, you paddle along below sandstone banks that soon grow into cliffs, and you return to deserted beaches.

The walk starts at the TURN-OFF to **Gardiki Castle**.

Follow the road to the CASTLE (**10min**). Just under 20 minutes later, bear left on the road to **Mesavrisi**. Reaching the beach and the causeway of dunes at the **Korission Lagoon** (**50min**), continue to the left — either along **Halikouna Beach** (Picnic 20a) or the parallel track.

When you reach the FISH FARM and the CANAL joining the so-called 'lake' to the sea (**1h45min**), cross the canal in the setting shown on page 120 (but the bridge may have changed). Then follow the sandy path into scrub (now referring to the map on pages 118-119). The path veers towards the lagoon and follows it for five minutes. Then, without warning, just before a line of poles in the lagoon, it swings right, back into the scrub (take care not to continue along the side of the lagoon). Soon a disused track comes underfoot. Emerging from the scrub, climb over the dunes, meandering through clumps of juniper and overlooking a landscape very unlike the olive-clad hills of the rest of Corfu: a lagoon trimmed in sedge and a countryside sparingly sprinkled with cottages.

On coming to the SEA (**2h20min**), head left towards Ag Georgios, passing **Issos Beach** (Picnic 20b). Follow the road through **Ag Georgios** then, just past the sign-posted turn-off to Argirades, descend to **Golden Beach** (**3h10min**). *(Shorter walk 1 leaves via the Argirades turn-off; Shorter walk 2 joins here.)* Head left along the beach, sometimes scrambling over rocks. After 50 minutes you pass the holiday village of **Santa Barbara** (**4h**). Further along this relatively-deserted coast, you round a rocky PROMONTORY (**4h45min**), a sheltered swimming spot with a number of small fishing boats. Head over to the small BRICK FISHERMEN'S SHELTER at the back of this beach and, keeping the shelter on your left, start up the track away from the beach. A couple of minutes along, you join two more tracks ascending from the beach. Climbing, you have a beautiful view of a near-deserted beach further along the coast. A steep climb brings you up to a JUNCTION at an olive grove (**5h15min**).

Bear left and then immediately right downhill on a wider, stony track, passing a chapel off to the right. Ignore any side-tracks. Join the SANTA BARBARA ROAD, and head right, crossing the bypass. Entering **Perivoli**, keep left (but *not* sharp left) at a junction 500m from the bypass. At the junction in front of the church belfry, go left again on the main road for a couple of minutes, to the BUS STOP (**6h10min**) by the cafés.

Walk 21: KAVOS • MONI PANAGIA • KANOULA BEACH • AG GORDIS BEACH • PALEOCHORI

Distance/time: 10km/6.2mi; 3h15min

Grade: moderate, with ascents/descents of about 200m/650ft. Care is needed occasionally, clambering over rocks.

Equipment: walking boots or stout shoes, sunhat, sunglasses, suncream, long-sleeved shirt, long trousers, raingear, swimwear, picnic, plenty of water

How to get there: 🚌 to Kavos; journey time 1h45min
To return: 🚌 from Paleochori (recheck departure time, as these bus times depend on school holidays); journey time 1h50min.

Short walk: Kavos — Moni Panagia — Kanoula Beach — Kavos: 8km/5mi; 2h20min. Easy ascents/descents of 100m/330ft; equipment and access as main walk; return on the same bus. Or 🚗 to/from Kavos: motorists should continue through the village and park at the side of the track to the monastery (see map), saving a total of 15min. Equipment and access as above. Follow the main walk to Kanoula Beach, then return on the beach track, keeping right uphill at the fork. A little over five minutes up, rejoin your outward track to the monastery, and turn left for Kavos. *Strongly recommended for beginners.*

Alternative walk: Kavos — Moni Panagia — Kanoula Beach — Spartera — Kavos: 10.8km/6.8mi; 3h40min. Grade and equipment as main walk. 🚌 or 🚗 to Kavos. Follow the main walk to the 1h30min-point. Walk along Kanoula Beach, climbing over an outcrop of rock, and continue to a track which leaves the beach from the far end. Follow this uphill and turn right at the first junction. Climb steeply for about 20 minutes, with fine views back over the beach. Less than an hour up from the beach turn right on the country road linking Kavos and Neochori. In a few minutes you reach the small village of Spartera. Follow the main road round to the right and continue for just over 2km, to a T-junction. Turn left here, back to Kavos.

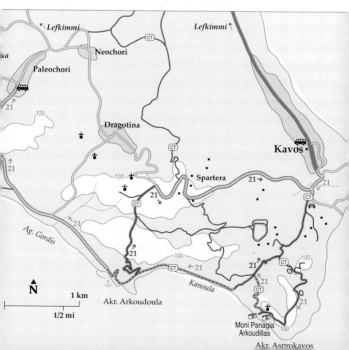

At the tip of the island, in a neighbourhood of holly oaks and cypresses, lie the remains of a fortified monastery — Moni Panagia Arkoudillas. This romantic ruin sits back just out of sight of the beautifully-eroded cliffs of Cape Asprokavos. The multitude of names scrawled on the monastery walls indicates that this is probably the most walked (or cycled) track on Corfu. For the locals however, the only interest this point holds is for shooting. Don't expect to see any birds around.

Get off the bus at the last stop in **Kavos**. **Start out** by keeping ahead on the main road, passing the MEDICAL CENTRE (which should be on your right when you alight from the bus.) At the JUNCTION (**5min**), turn right. A minute later cross a bridge, then follow the road to the left. Barely one minute further on, leave the road and turn right on a gravel and concrete TRACK SIGNPOSTED FOR MONI PANAGIA. There should also be some indication that the Corfu Trail starts here. This broad track takes you straight to the monastery. In the first few minutes ignore turn-offs to the left then the right. And within the following 10 minutes ignore two more tracks off to the right. *(The Short walk will return later along the second track.)*

Pass a DUMP at the right of the track (**45min**); at the

Moni Panagia Arkoudillas. This photograph was taken several years ago, when there were still bells in the belfry. The Short walk to the monastery is recommended for everyone, and would round off Car tour 4 perfectly.

fork five minutes later, keep right. You rise in the shade of a pretty oak wood, one of the few surviving on the island. Vines hang from the trees. But unfortunately there's another DUMP to pass, this one at the left of the track. Approaching the monastery, the track runs along the clifftops, which are hidden by vegetation. There are superb views along the dazzling white cliffs. *(If you scramble up to the edge of the cliff for a better view, do so with the utmost care! These cliffs crumble away easily!)*

Five minutes from the fork, **Moni Panagia** (**55min**) suddenly appears, quite close to the cliff-top, in a clump of cypress trees below the track. Inside the walls are two chapels, both now ruined. Remains of stairways and walls add to the charm of the site, the more so in spring and autumn when speckled with wild flowers. Take the path on the far side of the track, into the trees. It's overgrown and involves a lot of bending and ducking, but this short foray only takes two minutes. Fork right after 20-25m/yds; the path becomes clearer and follows the edge of the cliff, revealing a spectacular view over Kanoula Beach, which you will visit later.

Return to the *moni* and follow the track as it winds down through this enchanting forest, where the olive groves are being swallowed up by kermes oaks. Minutes downhill, the track ends at a T-junction with a path (the path to the right is so overgrown you may not see it). Head *left* for the beach: shove your way through scrub — the path is always clear. Five minutes down, cross a stream bed, then scramble up through scrub to a CONCRETE ROAD (**1h25min**) and turn left immediately; five minutes later you're on deserted **Kanoula Beach** (**1h30min**). *(From here the Short walk returns up the concrete road, keeping straight uphill at the fork.)*

The main walk continues along the broad sweep of the bay, towards the cape. Amongst the seashore rocks, you come across rock samphire *(Crithmum maritimum)*, a strange-smelling plant with blue-to-green fleshy leaves. Around 25 minutes along the beach, you pass below a track, but remain along the shoreline. Skirting a rocky headland, soon come to a small harbour with a number of fishing boats. Climb over some large boulders to reach a parking area and a road (**2h15min**). Follow the road behind **Ag Gordis Beach** or walk along the shore. After 20 minutes, at a road junction, continue 2.2km straight on to **Paleochori** (**3h15min**) — or turn right uphill, to walk 1.7km to **Dragotina** (**3h15min**).

BUS TIMETABLES

Note that these timetables were valid during the peak season at press date.
On either side of summer they may vary, cuts being made in mid-
September and October (when there may be only a skeleton service
until May). Buses are run by KTEL; their website, www.ktelkerkyras.gr,
has an easily-printed list of all services on the island. You can also
telephone for timetable information: 26610 28900/28920/28928.
There may be more frequent services than those shown here, which
were taken from the KTEL website just before press date. It is always
worth checking to see if more (or fewer!) buses are running; changes
to services are common. *For all buses except those with a frequent service,*
check and recheck both departure and return times at the bus station.

The timetables on the following pages make reference to two bus
stations. 'Station 1' is the terminal at the front of San Rocco Square/
Platia Georgiou Theotoki (blue suburban buses for the nearby resorts
both north and south of Corfu Town, ie Dasia, Potamos, Benitses,
etc); 'Station 2' is the New Fortress Square station, near the old port.
These green KTEL buses go to all other destinations on the island.
Both stations have timetables posted on site. Station 2 has a printed
giveaway timetable as well, but it only covers the main tourist centres.
(Timetables are also printed in tourist newspapers and leaflets.)

When catching a bus from Station 2, always arrive 15 minutes
early; it will take you that long to find your bus — the station is fairly
chaotic, especially in high season. Moreover, the bus conductors and
drivers at Station 2 seem to change daily, so they are not always a
reliable source of information! Remember this, when you go to
confirm and reconfirm times for your return bus: the staff very often
cannot remember, and so they make a guess — and get it wrong! Be
sure to recheck return times before setting out *with the bus conduc-
tor/driver with whom you make the outward journey.*

Acharavi (Station 2). See Timetable 9
Achilleion (Bus No 10, Station 1). Departs 07.00, 10.00, 12.00,
14.00, 17.00, 20.00 (Mon-Sat); departs 09.00, 13.00, 17.00, 19.00
(Sun/holidays). Returns 20 minutes later
Afionas (Station 2). See Timetable 10
Afra (Bus No 8, Station 1). Departs 06.15, 07.10, 08.00, 09.00,
11.00, 12.30, 13.15, 14.15, 15.15, 17.00, 19.10, 21.00, 22.30
(Mon-Sat); departs 08.00, 11.00, 13.00, 15.15, 18.00, 20.00
(Sun/holidays). Returns 20 minutes later
Ag Georgios Beach (Station 2). See Timetable 7
Ag Gordis (Station 2). See Timetable 4
Ag Ioannis (Station 2). See Timetable 5
Ag Martinos (Station 2). Departs 05.30, 13.30 (Mon-Sat only).
Returns 06.50, 14.50 (Mon-Sat only). Journey time 1h20min
Ag Mattheos (Station 2). Departs 06.15, 11.45, 14.30, 17.30 (Mon-
Fri); departs 06.15, 13.00 (Sat). Returns 06.45, 12.45, 15.30, 18.30
(Mon-Fri); returns 07.00, 14.00 (Sat). Journey time 45min
Ag Pandelimonas (Station 2). Departs 05.00, 14.00 (Mon-Sat only).
Returns 06.00, 15.30 (Mon-Sat only). Journey time 1h30min
Ag Stefanos (near Arilas) (Station 2). See Timetable 8
Ag Stefanos (near Kouloura) (Station 2). See Timetable 11
Alepou (Bus No 14, Station 1). Departs 08.15, 13.50, 17.15, 20.00
(Mon-Sat); departs 10.00, 13.50, 18.15 (Sun). Returns 20min later
Ano Garouna (Station 2). Departs 05.00, 06.30, 12.30, 15.15 (Mon-
Sat only). Returns 06.15, 07,10, 13.10, 15.55 (Mon-Sat only).
Journey time 40min

Ag Ilias (Station 2). See Timetable 11

Argirades (Station 2). See Timetables 2 and 7

Arilas (Station 2). See Timetable 10

Arkadades (Station 2). See Timetable 8

Armenades (Station 2). Departs 06.30, 13.30 (Mon-Sat only). Returns 07.30, 14.30 (Mon-Sat only). Journey time 1h05min

Avliotes (Station 2). See Timetable 8

Benitses (Bus No 6, Station 1). Departs 06.45, 08.00, 09.15, 10.30, 11.45, 13.30, 14.30, 15.45, 17.00, 18.15, 19.30, 20.45, 22.00 (Mon-Sat; fewer buses Sat pm); departs 08.30, 10.30, 12.30, 14.30, 17.00, 20.00 (Sun/hols). Returns 30mins later.

Dasia (Bus No 7, Station 1). Departs from 07.00 to 22.00 every half hour (daily). Returns 30 minutes later.

Doukades turn-off (Station 2). See Timetable 1; times approximately as Paleokastritsa

Episkepsis (Station 2). Departs 05.30, 14.00 (Mon-Sat only). Returns 07.15, 15.45 (Mon-Sat only). Journey time 1h15min

Ermones (Station 2). See Timetable 6

Gastouri (Bus No 10, Station 1). As Archilleion

Gianades (Station 2). Departs 06.30, 14.30 (Mon-Sat only). Returns 07.00, 15.00 (Mon Sat only). Journey time 35min

Glyfada (Station 2). See Timetable 5

Gouvia (Bus No 7, Station 1). As Dasia

Hlomos (Station 2). Departs 05.00, 14.15 (Mon-Sat only). Returns 06.45, 15.15 (Mon-Sat only). Journey time 1h

Ipsos (Station 2). See Timetable 12

Kalami turn-off (Station 2). See Timetable 11

Kanoni (Bus No 2, Station 1). Departs Mon-Fri: 06.30-22.00 every 30min; Sat: 06.30-14.30 every 30min, then every hour; Sun: 09.30-21.30 every hour; corresponding returns every 30min or every hour

Karoussades (Station 2). Departs 05.45, 09.00, 11.00, 14.00 (Mon-Sat); departs 09.30 (Sun). Returns 07.00, 10.15, 12.15, 15.00, 17.00 (Mon-Sat); returns 16.00 (Sun). Journey time 1h10min

Kassiopi (Station 2). See Timetables 11, 13

Kastellani (Station 2). See Timetable 4.

Kavadades/Magoulades junction (Station 2). See Timetable 10; times as Magoulades

Kavos (Station 2). See Timetable 2

Khoroepiskopi (Station 2). See Timetable 9

Kontokali (Bus No 7, Station 1). As Dasia

Korakades (Station 2). Departs 05.00, 13.30 (Mon-Sat only). Returns 06.30, 15.00 (Mon-Sat only). Journey time 1h

Korakiana (Station 2). Departs 06.45, 08.30, 12.15, 16.00 (Mon-Sat). Returns 07.15, 09.00, 12.45, 16.30. Journey time 25min

Krini (Station 2). Departs 07.00, 14.50 (Mon-Sat only). Returns 07.05, 15.30 (Mon-Sat only). Journey time 1h

Lafki (Station 2). Departs 04.45, 14.00 (Mon-Sat only). Returns 06.55, 16.10 (Mon-Sat only). Journey time 2h10min

Lefkimmi (Station 2). See Timetable 2

Liapades (Station 2). Departs 06.45, 14.00 (Mon-Sat only). Returns 07.15, 14.00 (Mon-Sat only). Journey time 35min

Loutses (Station 2). See Timetable 11

Magoulades (Station 2). See Timetable 10. Departures also via Armenades as above

Makrades (Station 2). Departs 06.30, 16.45 (Mon-Sat only). Returns 07.00, 14.30. Journey time 50min.

Messongi (Station 2). See Timetables 2, 3

Nimfes (Station 2). Departs 05.45, 13.45 (Mon-Sat only). Returns 06.30, 15.00 (Mon-Sat only). Journey time 50min

Nissaki (Station 2). See Timetable 11

Paleochori (Station 2). Scheduling variable; check times at station

Paleokastritsa (Station 2). See Timetable 1

Perama (Bus No 6, Station 1). As No 6 Bus to Benitses (see above)

Perivoli (Station 2). See Timetable 2

Peroulades (Station 2). See Timetable 8

Porta (Station 2). Departs 06.15, 12.15 (Mon-Sat only). Returns 07.15, 14.15 (Mon-Sat only). Journey time 1h10min

Prinilas (Station 2). Departs 06.15, 13.30 (Mon-Sat only). Returns 07.15, 14.30 (Mon-Sat only). Journey time 1h

Pyrgi (Station 2). See Timetable 12

Roda (Station 2). See Timetables 9, 13

Sfakera (Station 2). Roda bus; see Timetable 9; times approximately as for Roda

Sgombou (Station 2). See Timetable 1; times approximately as for Tsavros

Sidari (Station 2). See Timetables 8, 13

Sinarades (Station 2). See Timetable 4

Sokraki (Station 2). Departs 05.00, 14.00 (Mon-Sat only). Returns 06.00, 15.30 (Mon-Sat only). Journey time 1h25min

Spartera (Station 2). Departs 05.00, 15.00 (Mon-Sat only). Returns 06.15, 16.30. Journey time 1h25min

Spartilas (Station 2). Departs 05.30, 14.00 (Mon-Sat only). Returns 08.00, 16.30 (Mon-Sat only). Journey time 40min

Stavros (Station 2). As Strongili

Strinilas (Station 2). See Lafki bus. Journey time approx. 1h30min

Strongili (Station 2). Departs 06.00, 08.30, 12.30, 15.00, 17.30 (Mon-Fri); departs 07.00, 13.00 (Sat). Returns 07.00, 09.30, 13.30, 16.00, 18.30 (Mon-Fri); returns 08.00, 14.00 (Sat). Journey time 1h

Tembloni (Bus No 4, Station 1). Departs 06.40, 14.30 (Mon-Sat only). Returns 06.50,14.50

Troumpeta (Station 2). See Timetable 9

Tsavros (Station 2). See Timetable 1

Variapatades (Station 2). Departs 06.45, 13.00, 14.30, 16.30, 20.00 (Mon-Fri); departs 08.00, 14.30 (Sat). Returns 07.15, 13.30, 15.00, 17.00, 20.30 (Mon-Fri); returns 08.30, 15.00 (Sat). Journey time 35min

Vassili (Bus No 3, Station 1). Departs daily 07.30 to 20.30 every 30 minutes. Return journeys every 30 minutes

Vatos (Station 2). See Timetable 5

Vitalades (Station 2). Departs 05.45 (Mon-Sat only). Returns 07.15 (Mon-Sat only). Journey time 1h10min

1 Corfu • Tsavros • Paleokastritsa (also Sgombou, Doukades turn-off)

Monday to Saturday			*Sundays and holidays*		
Corfu	Tsavros	Paleokastritsa	Corfu	Tsavros	Paleokastritsa
08.30	08.50	09.15	10.30	10.50	11.05
09.00	09.20	09.45	12.00	12.20	12.35
10.00	10.20	10.45	16.00	16.20	16.35
11.00	11.20	11.45	18.00	18.20	18.35
12.00	12.20	12.45			
13.00	13.20	13.45			
14.15	14.35	15.00			
16.00	16.20	16.45			
16.30	16.50	17.15			
17.00	17.20	17.45			
18.00	18.20	18.45			
19.00	19.20	19.45			

RETURN BUSES

Monday to Saturday			*Sundays and holidays*		
Paleokastritsa	Tsavros	Corfu	Paleokastritsa	Tsavros	Corfu
09.15	09.30	09.50	11.15	11.30	11.50
09.45	10.00	10.20	12.45	13.00	13.20
10.45	11.00	11.20	16.45	17.00	17.20
11.45	12.00	12.20	18.45	19.00	19.20
12.45	13.00	13.20			
13.45	14.00	14.20			
15.00	15.15	15.35			
16.45	17.00	17.20			
17.15	17.30	17.50			
17.45	18.00	18.20			
18.45	19.00	19.20			
19.45	20.00	20.20			

2 Corfu • Messongi • Argirades • Perivoli • Lefkimmi • Kavos

Daily (but only two buses on Sundays)					
Corfu	Messongi	Argirades	Perivoli	Lefkimmi	Kavos
06.15*	06.50*	07.05*	07.20*	07.35*	07.55*
08.15+*	08.50+*	09.05+*	09.20+*	09.35+*	09.55+*
09.30‡•	10.05‡•	10.20‡•	10.35‡•	10.50‡•	11.10‡•
10.00+*	10.35+*	10.50+*	11.05+*	11.20+*	11.40+*
11.30*	12.05*	12.20*	12.35*	12.50*	13.10*
12.45+*	13.20+*	13.35+*	13.50+*	14.05+*	14.25+*
14.00*	14.35*	14.50*	15.05*	15.20*	15.40*
15.30*	16.05*	16.20*	16.35*	16.50*	17.10*
16.30•	17.05•	17.20•	17.35•	17.50•	18.10•
17.45*	18.20*	18.35*	18.50*	19.05*	19.25*
20.30*	21.05*	21.20*	21.35*	21.50*	22.10*

RETURN BUSES

Kavos	Lefkimmi	Perivoli	Argirades	Messongi	Corfu
07.45*	08.05*	08.20*	08.25*	08.50*	09.25*
09.45+*	10.05+*	10.20+*	10.25+*	10.50+*	11.25+*
11.00‡•	11.20‡•	11.35‡•	11.50‡•	12.05‡•	12.40‡•
11.30+*	11.50+*	12.05+*	12.20+*	13.35+*	14.10+*
13.00*	13.20*	13.35*	13.50*	14.05*	14.40*
14.15+*	14.35+*	14.50+*	15.05+*	15.20+*	15.55+*
15.30*	15.50*	16.05*	16.20*	16.35*	17.10*
17.00*	17.20*	17.35*	17.50*	18.05*	18.40*
18.00*	18.20*	18.35•	18.50•	19.05•	19.40•
19.00*	19.20*	19.35*	19.50*	20.05*	20.40*
22.00	22.20	22.35	22.50	23.05	23.40

+not Saturdays; *not Sundays; • only Sundays; ‡not Monday-Friday

3 Corfu • Benitses • Messongi

Monday to Saturday

Corfu	Benitses	Messongi	Messongi	Benitses	Corfu
09.00	09.25	09.40	07.00*	07.15*	07.40*
09.15	09.40	09.55	07.20*	07.35*	08.00*
10.00**	10.25**	10.40**	08.45	09.00	09.25
11.00*	11.25*	11.40*	10.00**	10.15**	10.40**
11.30	11.55	12.10	10.20**	10.35**	11.00**
12.45	13.10	13.25	11.45	12.00	12.25
14.00	14.25	14.40	12.45**	13.00**	13.25**
14.30**	14.55**	15.10**	13.45	14.00	14.25
15.30	15.55	16.10	15.00**	15.15**	15.40**
16.30	16.55	17.10	16.00**	16.15**	16.40**
17.45	18.10	18.25	16.45	17.00	17.25
19.00	19.25	19.40	17.45	18.00	18.25
20.30	20.55	21.10	19.45**	20.00**	20.25**
21.30**	21.55**	22.10**	21.45	22.00	22.25

*Saturdays only; **not Saturdays

Sundays and holidays

Corfu	Benitses	Messongi	Messongi	Benitses	Corfu
09.00	09.25	09.40	10.15	10.30	10.55
09.30	09.55	10.15	11.45	12.00	12.25
12.00	12.25	12.40	16.45	17.00	17.25
15.30	15.55	16.10	17.45	18.00	18.25
19.30	19.55	20.10	21.45	22.00	22.25

4 Corfu • Sinarades (via Kastellani) • Ag Gordis

Monday to Saturday

Corfu	Sinarades	Ag Gordis	Ag Gordis	Sinarades	Corfu
08.15	08.45	08.55	09.00	09.10	09.40
09.15	09.45	09.55	10.00	10.10	10.40
11.00*	11.30*	11.35*	11.45*	11.55*	12.25*
13.00	13.30	13.35	13.45	13.55	14.25
14.45	15.15	15.25	15.15	15.25	15.55
17.30	18.00	18.10	18.15	18.25	19.05
20.00	20.30	20.40	21.15	21.25	22.05

Sundays and holidays

Corfu	Sinarades	Ag Gordis	Ag Gordis	Sinarades	Corfu
11.30	12.00	12.10	12.15§	12.25§	12.55§
17.30	18.00	18.10	18.15§	18.25§	18.55§

*Not Saturdays

5 Corfu • Vatos (via Ag Ioannis) • Glyfada

Monday to Saturday			Sun/holidays		
Corfu	Vatos	Glyfada	Corfu	Vatos	Glyfada
09.00	09.30	09.40	11.30	12.00	12.10
11.00	11.30	11.40	13.00	13.30	13.40
13.00	13.30	13.40	16.00	16.30	16.40
14.30	15.00	15.10	17.30	18.00	18.10
16.00	16.30	16.40			
17.30	18.00	18.10			
20.30	21.00	21.10			

RETURN BUSES

Monday to Saturday			Sun/holidays		
Glyfada	Vatos	Corfu	Glyfada	Vatos	Corfu
09.45	09.55	10.25	12.15	12.25	12.55
11.45	11.55	12.25	13.45	13.55	14.25
13.45	13.55	14.25	16.45	16.55	17.25
15.15	15.25	15.55	18.15	18.25	18.55
16.45	16.55	17.25			
18.15	18.25	18.55			
21.15	21.25	21.55			

6 Corfu • Ermones • Corfu

Mon-Sat: Departs Corfu 09.00, 11.00, 12.00 (not Sat), 14.30, 16.00, 17.30, 20.30; returns from Ermones 10.00, 11.55, 12.35 (not Sat), 13.35, 15.00, 16.30, 18.10, 21.00; *Sundays:* Departs Corfu 11.30, 16.00; returns from Ermones 12.25, 16.30; journey time 35min.

7 Corfu • Ag Georgios Beach (near Argirades)

Mon-Fri: Departs Corfu 06.15, 09.00, 13.30, 16.15; returns from Ag Georgios 07.20, 10.15, 14.45, 17.30; *Saturdays:* Departs Corfu 09.00, 16.15; returns from Ag Georgios 10.15, 17.30; *no Sunday buses;* journey time about 1h

8 Corfu • Arkadades • Sidari • Peroulades • Avliotes • Ag Stefanos

Corfu	Arkadades	Sidari	Peroulades	Avliotes	Ag Stefanos
		Monday to Saturday			
05.00	05.40	06.10	06.15	06.25	06.35
08.30	09.10	09.40	09.45	09.55	10.05
12.00*	12.40*	13.10*	13.15*	13.25*	13.35*
14.00	14.40	15.10	15.15	15.25	15.35
16.00	16.40	17.10	17.15	17.25	17.35
		Sundays and holidays			
11.15	11.55	12.25	12.30	12.40	12.45
16.30	17.10	17.40	17.45	17.55	18.05

RETURN BUSES

Ag Stefanos	Avliotes	Peroulades	Sidari	Arkadades	Corfu
		Monday to Saturday			
06.25	06.35	06.45	06.50	07.20	08.00
09.05*	09.15*	09.25*	09.30*	10.00*	10.40*
10.15	10.25	10.35	10.40	11.10	11.50
13.40*	13.50*	14.00*	14.05*	14.35*	15.15*
15.35	15.45	15.55	16.00	16.30	17.10
17.35	17.45	17.55	18.00	18.30	19.10
		Sundays and holidays — only one bus			
16.50	17.00	17.10	17.15	17.45	18.25

*not Saturdays

9 Corfu • Troumpeta • Khoroepiskopi • Roda • Acharavi

Corfu	Troumpeta	Khoroepiskopi	Roda	Acharavi
		Monday to Saturday		
08.15*	08.45*	08.55*	09.15*	09.30*
08.30	09.00	09.10	09.30	09.45
11.00	11.30	11.40	12.00	12.15
13.45	14.15	14.25	14.45	15.00
16.00	16.30	16.40	17.00	17.15
18.30	19.00	19.10	19.30	19.45
20.30	21.00	21.10	21.30	21.45
		Sundays and holidays — only one bus		
09.30	10.00	10.10	10.30	10.45

RETURN BUSES

Acharavi	Roda	Khoroepiskopi	Troumpeta	Corfu
		Monday to Saturday		
07.00	07.15	07.50	08.00	08.30
09.30*	09.45*	10.05*	10.15*	10.45*
12.15	12.30	12.50	13.00	13.30
15.30	15.45	16.05	16.15	16.45
17.15	17.30	17.50	18.00	18.30
19.40	19.55	20.15	20.25	20.55
21.45	22.00	22.20	22.30	23.00
		Sundays and holidays — only one bus		
17.15	17.30	17.50	18.00	18.30

*Not Saturdays

10 Corfu • Magoulades • Afionas

Monday to Saturday only							
Corfu	Magoulades	Afionas	Arilas	Afionas	Arilas	Magoulades	Corfu
05.00	06.05	06.20	06.40	08.50	09.05	09.15	10.20
13.45	15.50	16.10	16.25	15.15	15.30	15.40	16.45

11 Corfu • Nissaki • Kalami turn-off • Kassiopi • Ag Ilias+ • Loutses+

Journey times (approximate): Corfu to Nissaki 40min; Nissaki to Kalami turn-off 15min; Kalami turn-off to Ag Stefanos turn-off 5min; Ag Stefanos turn-off to Kassiopi 5min; Kassiopi to Ag Ilias 10min; Ag Ilias to Loutses 10min

Monday to Saturday: Departs Corfu 05.30*+, 06.00•, 08.30, 09.00, 10.00, 11.00, 12.15, 14.30+, 16.00, 16.30 18.30, 20.00
Sundays and holidays: Departs Corfu 09.30, 10.00, 16.30

RETURN BUSES
Monday to Saturday: Departs Kassiopi 07.00*, 07.30•, 10.00, 11.15, 12.15, 13.45, 16.15, 17.45, 19.45
Sundays and holidays: Departs Kassiopi 17.05; departs Nissaki for Corfu 10.45 also

+On Mon, Wed, Fri *only,* these buses go on to/depart from Loutses; they depart Loutses for Corfu on Mon, Wed, Fri *only* at 06.45 and 16.00.
*Not Saturdays; •Only Saturdays

12 Corfu • Pyrgi/Ipsos

Monday to Saturday: Departs Corfu 05.30*, 06.00•, 08.30, 09.00, 09.30, 10.00, 11.00, 11.30, 12.15, 14.00*, 14.30, 15.30, 16.00, 16.30, 17.15, 18.30, 19.00, 20.00, 21.30; returns from Pyrgi/Ipsos 07.30, 08.00•, 09.15*, 10.00, 10.40, 11.50, 12.00, 12.50, 13.10*, 14.20*, 16.00, 17.00, 18.20, 19.30, 20.20, 21.00, 22.00
Sundays and holidays: Departs Corfu 09.30, 10.00, 11.30, 14.00, 15.30, 16.30, 18.30, 20.00; returns from Pyrgi/Ipsos 10.30, 11.00, 12.00, 14.30, 16.090, 17.00, 17.30, 17.45, 19.00, 20.30
*Not Saturdays; •Only Saturdays

13 Kassiopi • Roda • Sidari

Monday to Saturday					
Kassiopi	Roda	Sidari	Sidari	Roda	Kassiopi
09.30	09.55	10.15	10.15	10.35	11.00
11.30	11.55	12.15	12.15	12.35	13.00
14.30	14.55	15.15	15.15	15.35	16.00
16.00	16.25	16.45	16.45	17.05	17.30
Sundays and holidays					
Kassiopi	Roda	Sidari	Sidari	Roda	Kassiopi
11.15	11.40	12.00	10.30	10.50	11.15
16.30	16.55	17.15	16.00	16.20	16.45

● Index

Geographical names comprise the only entries in this Index. For other entries, see Contents, page 3. **Bold type** indicates a photograph; *italic* type a map (*TM* refers to the large-scale *walking map* on the reverse of the touring map). See separate index on page 128 for bus destinations and timetables. The accent ´ indicates the syllable to be stressed.

Acharávi 20, 24, 128
Achílleion Palace, Gardens 30, 34, 36, 128
Afiónas **10-11**, 14, 26, 29, **89**, *90-91*, 128
Ag Arsénious (chapel) 57, **58-59**, *TM*
Ag Déka (village and mountain) 35, **36**, **110**, 111, 112, *113*, 114
Ag Dimítrios 117, *118-119*
Ag Geórgios (near Afiónas) 14, 26, 29, *90-91*
Ag. Geórgios (near Argirades) *118-119*, 123, 124, 128
Ag. Georgios (near Perivoli) *118-119*, 123, 124
Ag Geórgios (mountain, near Vátos) *108-109*
Ag Geórgiou (bay, near Afiónas) 26, 29, 32, **87**, 88, 89, *90-91*
Ag Górdis (resort west of Corfu Town) 30, 34, 128
Ag Górdis (beach on the west side of Cape Kavos) *125*, 127
Ag Ilias 22, *47*, 130
Ag Iliódoros (cape) 94, *100-101*
Ag Márkos 21
Ag Matthéos (village and mountain) **15**, **24**, 35, 40, **120**, 121, *122*, 128
Ag Noufúres (monastery) 98, **99**
Ag Pandelímonas 24, 128
Ag Siméon (chapel) 98, *100-101*, **102**, 103
Ag Spirídon 12, 24, *47*, 49
Ag Stéfanos (near Arílas) 28, *83*, 128
(near Kouloúra) 22, 57, 60, 128, *TM*
Ag Theódori 34, 40
Ag Triáda (monastery) 76, 78, *TM*
Agni (cove) 58, *TM*
Almíros 24, *47*, 49
Anapaftíria 75, *TM*
Angelókastro (castle ruins) 15, 30, 31, *90-91*, 92
Ano Garoúna 30, 34, 111, 112, *113*,
Ano Messongí 35, 36, 39, *118-119*, 123
Ano Períthia (*see* Perithia, Ano)
Antiniótissa Lagoon 24, *47*, **48**
Arákli (mountain) 14, 92, *90-91*
Argirádes 35, 37, *118-119*, 123, 128

Arílas 26, 28, 128
Arílla (cape) **10-11**, 14, **28**, *90-91*
Arkadádes 26, 29, 129
Avliótes 28, 82 *83*, 85, 129

Barbáti 21
Bastatíka 39
Benítses 15, 36, 111, *113*, 114, 129
Bodholákos **23**, 50, 51, **50-1**, *TM*
Boukári 37, 117, *118-119*

Canal d'Amour 27
Corfu Town 20, 26, 30, 35
town plan 8-9

Dafnáta 35, *113*, 114, 115
Doukádes 15, 32, 98, *100-101*, 102, **103**
Dragotína 39, 125, *127*
Drástis (cape) 28, 82, *83*, **85**

Ekaterinis (cape) *47*, 49
Epískepsis **2**, **12**, 20, 24, 65, 69, 129, *TM*

Gardíki Castle 35, 39, 40, *122*, 123, 124
Garnelatíka (Nissaki) 53, 61, *TM*
Gastóuri 34, 129
Gavrolímni (pond) 15, 32, 97, 98, 99, *100-101*
Gianádes 94, 96, *100-101*, 129
Glyfáda 30, 33, 105, *108-109*, 110, 129
Golden Beach *118-119*, 123, 124
Gouviá 20, 105, *108-109*, 129

Halikoúna Beach 16, *122*, 124
Hlomós 16, 35, 37, **117**, *118-119*, 129

Imerólia 12, 22, 50, 52, *TM*
Ipsíli (monastery) **82**, *83*, 85
Ipsos (*see* Pyrgí/Ipsos)
Issós Beach **15**, 16, 35, 37, *118-119*, 124
Ithámi (monastery) 82, *83*, 85

Kaiser's Throne 33
Kalamáki Beach 65, 71, 75, *TM*
Kalámi 13, 21, 53, 57, 58, **60**, 129, *TM*

135

Kamináki Beach 53, 57, *TM*
Kanoula Beach *125,* 127
Karoussádes 27, 129
Kassiópi 12, 20, 22, **23**, 50, 52, 129, *TM*
Kastelláni 29, 129
Katávolos 13, **54**, 55, *TM*
Káto Garóuna 30, 34
Káto Spílion *118-119*
Kavadádes 129
Kávos 35, 38, *125,* 126, 129
Kendromádi 57, 60, *TM*
Kéndroma 21
Kerasiá Beach 57, 59, *TM*
Kiprianádes 26
Klimatiá 76, 78, *TM*
Komianáta 16, *113,* 114, 115, 116
Kontókali 20, 129
Korakádes 16, 37, 117, *118-119*, 120, 129
Korissíon Lagoon 16, 35, 37, 39, *118-119*, **120**, *122*, 123, 124
Kouloúra 13, 21, 53, 56, 57, *TM*
Kouspádes 35, 37, 117, *118-119*, 120
Kríni 31, *90-91*, 92, **93**, 129
Kritiká 39

Láfki 61, 64, 129, *TM*
Lake Korission (*see* Korission Lagoon)
Lakónes 14, **18-19**, 30, 31, 86, 87, *90-91*, 92
Lefkímmi 35, **38**, 129
Liapádes **18-19**, 32, 94, 95, *100-101*, **102**, 129, **cover**
Línia 36
Loútses 22, 65, 71, 75, 129, *TM*

Magouládes 82, *83,* 85, 129
Makrádes 30, 32, 88, *90-91*, 92
Mármaro (hills) 94, *100-101*
Méngoulas 61, *TM*
Mesavrísi 16, 39, *122,* 124
Messongí 35, 36, 117, *118-119*, 129
Mirtiótissa (beach and monastery) 15, 30, 33, 105, **106-107**, *108-109*, 110
Moraítika 36

Neochóri 39
Nímfes 14, 26, 27, 76, **77**, 129, *TM*
Nissáki 13, 20, 21, 53, 56, 57, 61, 65, 66, 129, *TM*
Nótos (cove) 117, *118-119,* 120

Pági 29, *90-91*
Paleochóri *125,* 127, 130
Paleokastrítsa **18-19**, 30, **31**, 86, *90-91*, 93, 94, 95, *100-101*, 130
Pálies Sínies 65, **68**, 75, *TM*
Panagía (monastery) *125,* **126,** 127
Pantokrátor (mountain and monastery) 20, **21**, 25, 65, 68, **70**, 71, 74, *TM*
Pantokrátor (monastery at Nímfes) 14, 76, **77**, *TM*

Pantokrátor (monastery on Mt Ag Déka) 111, 112, **110**
Pantokrátor (monastery on Mt Ag Mattheos) 121, *122*
Pantokrátor (chapel on Mt Stavrós) *113,* 114, **115**, 116
Paramóna 40
Pélekas 30, 33, 34
Pérama 35, 130
Períthia (Ano) 13, 20, 23, 61, **62-63, 64**, 65, 71, 75, 130, *TM*
Perivóli 35, 38, **40**, 117, *118-119,* 120, *122,* 123, 124, 130
Perouládes 26, 28, 82, *83,* **84**, 130
Petretí 16, 37, 117, *118-119*, 120
Pondikonísi (Mouse Island) **1**, 35
Port Timone **10-11**, 89, *90-91*
Pórta 53, 55, 61, 65, **67**, 130, *TM*
Prinílas *90-91*, 130
Proussádi (cove) 40
Pyrgí/Ipsos 20, 79, 81, 129, 130, *TM*

Róda 26, 27, 65, 70, 130, *TM*
Rópa Plain 15, 30, **32-33, 80**, 94, 96, *100-101*, 105, 107, *108-109*
Roú 53, 55, *TM*
Rovina Beach 94, *100-101*

Sánta Bárbara *118-119,* 124
Scotiní (pond) **105**, 106, *108-109*
Seki Bay 75, *TM*
Sfakerá 65, 70, 130, *TM*
Sgomboú 26, 94, 97, 98, *100-101*, 104, 130
Sgourádes 24
Sidári 26, 27, 130
Sinarádes 30, 34, 130
Skidí Beach 40
Skrípero 26
Sokráki 79, 80, 130, *TM*
Sparterá 39, *125*
Spartílas 14, 20, 25, 71, **78**, 79, 81, 130, *TM*
Stavrós (mountain) 35, *113,* 116, 130
Strinílas 13, 25, 65, 69, 130, *TM*
Strongilí 35, *113,* 114, 116, 130

Taxiárkhis (chapel) 71, 72, **73**, *TM*
Theapondinisi Islands 26, 27
Triálos 105, *108-109*
Trivouliáttica 97, 98, *100-101*, 104
Troumpéta (pass and hamlet) 14, 26, 29, 30, 32, 79, 130, *TM*
Tsavrós junction 20, 26, 29, 130

Valanío 26
Vassilátika *118-119,* 124
Vátos 33, 105, *108-109,* 130
Vígla 53, 56, *TM*
Viglatóuri 66, *TM*
Vístonas 32, 88, *90-91*
Vouniatádes 40